100 DAYS OF CREE

100 DAYS OF CREE

NEAL McLEOD

WITH AROK WOLVENGREY

University of Regina Press

Printed and bound in Canada at Friesens.

COVER AND TEXT DESIGN: Duncan Campbell, University of Regina Press
COPY EDITOR: Meaghan Craven
PROOFREADER: Katie Doke Sawatzky
COVER ART: "mashkihkiy-misatim" (medicine horse), 2015 by Neal McLeod. From the collection of Lee Maracle.
INTERIOR ILLUSTRATIONS: Neal McLeod.

Library and Archives Canada Cataloguing in Publication
McLeod, Neal, author
100 days of Cree / Neal McLeod with Arok Wolvengrey.

Issued in print and electronic formats.
Text in English; some text in Cree.
ISBN 978-0-88977-429-2 (paperback).—ISBN 978-0-88977-430-8 (pdf)

1. Cree language—Vocabulary. I. Wolvengrey, Arok, 1965-, author
II. Title. III. Title: One hundred days of Cree.
PM986.M36 2016   497'.97323   C2016-901247-6   C2016-901248-4

We acknowledge the support of the Canada Council for the Arts for our publishing program. We acknowledge the financial support of the Government of Canada. / Nous reconnaissons l'appui financier du gouvernement du Canada. This publication was made possible through Creative Saskatchewan's Creative Industries Production Grant Program.

To the memory of Freda Ahenakew,
Charlie Burns, Ida McLeod,
and Jermiah McLeod

CONTENTS

ACKNOWLEDGEMENTS

I am very thankful to the many people who have contributed to the development of this book: Barry Ahenakew, Derek Ahenakew, Sekwun Ahenakew, Guy Albert, Bob Badger, the late Charlie Burns, Mary Cardinal Collins (and her "old ladies"), Karen Chamakese, Bill Cook and John Cook for keeping the cool in Cree, Susan Cook, Treffrey Deerchild, Tessa Desnomie, Max Fineday, Wes Fineday, Cory Generoux, Wayne Goodspirit, Keith Goulet, kihci Chris Hunter (especially for his help with maskêko-Cree), Cheryl L'Hirondelle, Marlene L'Hirondelle, Russell Iron, Celina Jones, Bobby Kayseas (and his dad), Kevin Lewis, the late Âhâsiw Maskêko-Iskwêw, Sylvia McAdam (and her mother), George McLeod, the late Jermiah McLeod, Donald Meyer, Herman Michell, Denise Montour, Randy "Boyce" Morin, Joseph Naytowhow, Darren Okemaysim, John Quinney, Brenda Sanderson, Neil Sapp, Rosary Spence, Dorothy Thunder, the late Arsene Tootoosis, Celeste Tootoosis, Colby Tootoosis, Leona Tootoosis (and her daughter Lisa), Tyrone Tootoosis Sr., Caroline Utinowatum, the late Burton Vandall, Elaine Vandall, Shirley Williams, and Jhaik Windy Hair.

I would also like to thank my son, Cody Neal McLeod, for inspiring me to think of the next generation of Cree speakers.

I am very thankful for the many contributions of my friend Arok Wolvengrey, who thoroughly edited the work to make sure that everything, while interesting and creative at times, was also grammatically sound. I am also grateful to Arok for producing the Guide to Cree Pronunciation.

Last, I thank all of our ancestors, who kept our language alive through very difficult times. It is now our job to take care of it, for future generations.

INTRODUCTION

The book *100 Days of Cree* emerged organically, much of the material initially appearing as a series of Facebook posts. I was a latecomer to Facebook, and after being on it briefly, I began to post in Cree. Living away from my homeland of Saskatchewan, I found Facebook to be a very powerful way to connect with other Cree-speaking people and people interested in the Cree language. As I began to get more and more responses from my small posts in Cree, I had the idea of a large, ongoing project, wherein I would post at least ten words a day on a concentrated theme for one hundred days straight.

When I started this book, I remembered an Old Man at a round dance who said if we learned some Cree every day for a stretch of time, we would eventually know a great many words. There were times when I was working on this project that I felt I might stop, but the words of this Old Man, Mel Joseph, from the Whitefish Reserve in Saskatchewan, inspired me to finish.

In the middle of the project, on April 8, 2011, Freda Ahenakew entered the spirit world. She was one of the strongest living links to nôhkomipan ('my late grandmother') Ida McLeod. Together these two Cree woman helped standardize our writing system, leaving a great legacy for us to retrieve our language.

And so this book attempts to make a small contribution to the continued vitality of the Cree language, and to help provide people interested in the language to be able to use it to describe the world around them. The book tries to not only gather some of the classical vocabulary of the Cree language—for instance, three days are dedicated to horse terminology—but also to coin and develop words for contemporary life.

With respect to the classical vocabulary, I would like to acknowledge the important work of Leonard Bloomfield. Bloomfield collected stories of Cree speakers on the Sweetgrass Reserve in the Battlefords area of Saskatchewan in the 1920s and published these as *Plains Cree Texts* (as part of the Publications of the American Ethnological Society) in 1934. What makes these narratives important is that they were recorded with a great deal of accuracy, capturing the voices of our ancestors. They open a window in time, illustrating how the Cree (nêhiyawak) saw the world nearly a century ago. In *100 Days of Cree*, we look at words and phrases from several of these narratives, as they give us a way to study the terms in the context in which they were spoken rather than in isolation, as simply words on a blank page devoid of much of their meaning. As such, I have also been working on a retranslation of the narratives in *Plains Cree Texts*, hoping that this will contribute, at least in a small way, to the revitalization of the Cree language. In *100 Days of Cree*, we also look at words and phrases from David G. Mandelbaum's *The Plains Cree: An Ethnographic, Historical, and Comparative Study*, originally published as a dissertation in 1940, then reissued as a new edition in 1979 by the Canadian Plains Research Center (CPRC) at the University of Regina. CPRC has since become the University of Regina Press, and Mandelbaum's *The Plains Cree* remains in print.

With respect to the revitalization of the Cree language mentioned above, there was much discussion throughout this project about the use of Cree to describe the world in which we live today.

Terms were developed for things such as Internet use and computers, demonstrating the great flexibility and adaptability of the language. It is hoped these gathered terms will offer something to the new, large, emerging generation of Cree speakers, in whose minds and bodies the future of the language now rests.

Of course, there are some key differences between the original Facebook posts and this book. While the Facebook exchanges allowed for much conjecture (but also a lot of fun), I felt that to sharpen the material for a book, any terms of questionable accuracy should be dropped. I also felt I should expand upon the dialogue that introduced each theme discussed. So, I began to edit the lists again with my friend Arok Wolvengrey, adding words through additional research to help fill in any gaps we identified.

The work on this book demonstrated a few things to me. First, the Cree language is built upon a collective process and effort. I believe that the more we assist and help each other with learning the language, the stronger the language will be. Second, I was struck by the elasticity between the written and the oral forms of Cree—these forms complement each other, strengthen each other, and exist simultaneously with each other. Last, I learned there is a strong interest among younger people to learn and use Cree in their daily lives.

With this in mind, I have decided to donate all royalties received from the sale of this book to a student scholarship fund.

I am a poet, and in this book I have attempted to push the Cree language to its limits. To quote the old Cree expression, kâya pakicî! âhkamêyimo! ('Don't quit! Persevere!').

Neal McLeod

DAY 1

WORKING TOGETHER

One of the key things about learning a language is that people assist each other in the process. Unfortunately, there have been many ruptures and breaks in the threads of our language through time: residential schools, collective trauma, and the influence of television and mass communication. Some of us no longer have grandparents—mosômak and kôhkomak—who can guide us in the process of learning language and stories. We need the stories and philosophy to drive and fuel our understanding of the language. It is by a collective effort that we can bring the power of the echo of the voices of the Old Ones, and the old stories, into the contemporary age. As such, the theme for Day 1 is "working together," and the words below provide some vocabulary for this process.

wîcihitok 'help one another!'.

wîcihikowisi- 'to be helped by higher powers'. -ikowisi 'by the powers' is an important verb ending in Cree. The way this verb ending works is that it is connected to another verb that describes what the powers "do for us," or how we relate to the powers. This verb points to the inherently spiritual nature of the Cree language.

ê-mâmawi-atoskâtamahk 'we work on something together': the preverb mâmawi- 'together'; atoskâta 'work on it'.

kiskisomitok 'remind each other': kiskisi 'remember'; kiskisom 'remind him/her'; ito denotes reciprocity in the verb that precedes it.

kisêwâtisitotaw 'be kind and generous to someone': kisê- '(to be) kind'; (w)âtisi 'to be or live in such a way', as described by the stem that precedes.

minowâtisiw (maskêko-Cree) 's/he is generous': mino- 'good' (maskêko-Cree) and miyo- 'good' (Plains Cree); -(w)âtisi 'to be or live in such a way', as described by the stem that precedes.

mâtinamâkêw 's/he shares with everyone' (usually food).

kiskinohamaw 'teach someone': kiskino- 'to point, to guide'.

kêhtin 'treat him/her with respect'.

sîhkimitowin 'the process of encouraging each other': sîhkim 'encourage him/her'; again, the ending -ito, which denotes reciprocity; -win, an ending that converts some verbs into nouns.

The terms listed here can be augmented with additional meanings and dialectal variations. Stories, of course, animate the words and, most important, give a context for the meaning of the words in the language.

DAY 2

SKY

The sky is important in Cree stories and in the Cree language. Especially where I come from, in the land of kisiskâciwan-sîpiy (the Saskatchewan River), the sky is vibrant, full of colour and twisting forms. Many of the beings in Cree stories and beliefs dwell in the sky, such as the piyêsiwak (Thunder Beings) and of course all of the other birds. The sky-forms, such as clouds and developing weather patterns, originate in the sky. Throughout human history much of Cree pimâcihowin 'livelihood' has been derived from the sky.

kîsik 'sky'; has a cool downtown twang in Ojibwe: giizhig.

kîsikâw 'day', 'it is daylight'; literally, 'there is sky'.

payipwât the name of the legendary Cree-Assiniboine leader; literally, 'hole in the Dakota'. He had been captured as a child by the Dakota and was recaptured when he was about 15 years old. He was a 'hole in the Dakota', because apparently people thought that he knew the "playbook" of the Dakota, as it were. His first name was kîsikâw-awâsis, understood as 'Lightning Boy', but this name actually pointed to the sky. There was lightning the day he was born.

piyêsiw 'Thunderbird', 'Being of the sky'. My ancestor, the first McLeod, was named nîkân-isi 'the foremost being', which metaphorically refers to Thunderbird. I suppose that is why I have always been interested in the words of the sky.

pê-wâpan 'the coming of dawn'; wâpahki means 'when it is dawn', but also 'tomorrow'.

wâsaskotêpayin 'lightning'; wâh-wâstêpaniwin (maskêko-Cree). The ending -payi/-pani denotes sudden action and transformation. In my experience, this is one of the most important elements in the Cree language. The other stems in operation here are wâsaskotê- and wâstê-, both referring to 'light, bright light'; so, when the two elements are compounded, it means 'there is a rapid burst of light'.

pitihkwêw 'there is thunder' (maskêko-Cree). Interestingly, there is a place in Alberta called nipiy kâ-pitihkwêk (Sounding Lake). They say that this is where a Thunderbird was dragged into the lake by a water snake. I have also heard the stem pitihkwê- in reference to the random sounds of fighting.

kâ-šošopêhikanaskwahk 'the sky is full of colour' (maskêko-Cree); literally, 'when the clouds are painted'. This word is a beautiful rendering of the idea of a sky full of life and colour. It really refers to clouds and not the sky itself. This use of metaphor and indirect pointing is common in Cree.

wâsêyâw 'it is bright, shining', 'it is a bright sky'.

wâsêskwâstan 'the wind has cleared the sky'; -âstan is a verb ending that denotes action by the wind.

DAY 3

WATER

Water plays a key role in understanding our place in the world. Throughout our ceremonies, the life-giving power of water is honoured, and we have many songs to hold this importance in our collective memory. In recent years, many Indigenous women have brought attention to the importance of water by walking around bodies of water, including the Great Lakes, to honour the water and its life-giving gifts.

nipiy 'water'.

môskipê- 'to emerge from water'. With this word, I think of the horses that emerged from lakes like mihkomin-sâkahikan (Redberry Lake).

cikâstêpêsin 'Shadow Lying on the Water'; Chief of a band whose people later came to camp with people on my reserve, nihtâwikihcikanisihk 'at the good growing place' (James Smith Cree Nation). Let's look at this word's components: cikâstê(w) '[there is a] shadow'; -pê, a root meaning 'water' or 'liquid' when it occurs at the end of a word or is incorporated into the middle of a word; -sin, a verb ending indicating 'lying down'. This is an example of how one Cree word is like a line of poetry.

pîkahin okosisa Oral history from my reserve of this man kâ-kî-kiskiwêhikêt 'who prophesized' what would happen ôtê nîkânihk 'in the future'. He was also from cikâstêpêsin's band. The name pîkahin appears to be a classical Cree word that means 'to stir a liquid' (water implied).

pâwistik 'rapids'.

nâmonipêk 'James Bay'; literally, 'neighbour bay' (maskêko-Cree).

tâwic 'coast' (maskêko-Cree).

kihci-wînipêk- 'Hudson's Bay'; literally, 'the great dirty water', like Lake Winnipeg (wînipêk). Notice how when named in Cree the place and the history come to light in a completely different way. Imagine the kihci-wînipêk Trading Company. cah!

kwâpikê- 'to fetch water'.

kisiskâciwan-sîpiy '(North) Saskatchewan River'; literally, 'the fast flowing river'. I grew up near the place where the river forks.

DAY 4

HONOUR

I always remember the way my late father spoke of things, the way he spoke of history, and the way he spoke of the future. He often spoke of the way in which people conducted themselves, and ways that they should conduct themselves. Embedded within his stories and language was the idea of honour—which is certainly an old Cree idea and concept. Some would say that this is an old-fashioned idea, but I think there is a great deal of power in this old idea.

kistêyimitowin 'honour'. It really means 'thinking highly of one another' and represents the process of reciprocal honour and respect. Let's look at this word's components: kist- 'important, high'; -êyim 'to think of someone or something animate'; -ito 'reciprocal action' as indicated by the adjoined verb; -win 'a general process'. So you could translate this more literally as 'the process of holding each other in high regard'.

k-âsôhakaniyik otatoskêwin 'her/his work passes through generations'. This could be thought of as a way to describe someone's legacy. Once again, a lot of these words/phrases are like little poems.

okihcitâw 'worthy young man'. This word has been mistakenly translated as 'warrior' by anthropologists. It is both a noun and verb, meaning 'a provider' and 'to provide for people'. The implication is that there is a sense of honour in thinking of others. They say that in the old days the okihcitâwak, when they hunted, would eat last. Everyone else would eat first. Good motivation to be a good hunter! Today, I guess that would be like the guy who went to get the bucket of KFC and then had to eat last—he would be sure to come back with more than enough chicken!

kihcihtâkosiwi-nikamowin 'honour song'; literally, 'the high/important-sounding song'. But this one has been tricky; I remember hearing a different word for "honour song," which I can't quite remember. So this is one possibility suggested by a friend; another is askiy-nikamowin 'earth song'.

sôhkêyimowin 'bravery'. The old soldiers lived this value in combat. My mosôm Gabriel Vandall embodied this idea at the Battle of Juno Beach in 1944.

oskâpêyos Dialectically, this is a slightly twangy version of the more uptown oskâpêwis. Literally, 'a young man'—but in practical terms, it means 'a ceremonial helper'. I have often asked about the female version of this word. In *Nationhood Interrupted: Revitalizing nêhiyaw Legal Systems*, Sylvia McAdam (Saysewahum) refers to kâ-omîkwanisicik iskwêwak 'the feathered women', that is, 'feather-carriers; female helpers'.

ê-kwêskît 's/he turns around'. With this word, I was thinking of a way to say 'to regain honour'. We have all made mistakes, but perhaps when we turn our lives around, when we atone, then we move towards regaining our honour. The more I think about Cree, the more I appreciate its extensive use of metaphors and indirect pointing. This seems to free the language up to create space for symbolism—making Cree a natural language for poetry.

nimihtâtên 'I regret [something]'. From what I understand, there is no way to say "sorry" in Cree—all you can say is "I greatly regret" something. I see this as a relevant concept as we think about recovering honour—that is, by regretting, we move towards transforming our actions.

mistahi kî-okimâwiw 'he was a great chief'. This is how kâ-pîhtokêw-kîsikâw 'Coming Day' referred to wîhkasko-kisêyin 'Old Man Sweetgrass' in *Plains Cree Texts*. This phrase demonstrates the idea of honour through strong political leadership.

ê-âpahot 's/he regains honour'. This is a nice metaphorical extension of âpaho- 'to release oneself', 'to undo or reverse something', or 'to be absolved'.

DAY 5

SOUND

Cree culture and language rests in sound, and our bodies are the vehicles of this sound. This sound passes through us during our lifetimes, and gradually we accumulate this sound in our beings and pass this embodied being to others. Many Cree names invoke ideas of sound and the way in which they carry this sound through stories.

ê-kaskêyihtamo-nikamot 's/he sings a lonely song'—a song of longing, of loss, of being lonely. Could be used for a love song, when your heart aches for someone.

nêhiyawêwin 'Cree language'. But, if you were to get poetic, you could think of the word as 'an ongoing process of making Cree sound'. The first part of this word is nêhiyaw 'Cree, Cree person'. The second part of the stem nêhiyawê- 'speak Cree' is -awê. This common element occurring in the middle and end of words, especially names, means 'sound' or 'voice'. The parts before this stem describe the sound of the name or word. In this case, nêhiyawê seems to indicate 'precise speech' or 'skilled voice'. Sometimes another ending -mo occurs, indicating speech and language (as in Anishinaabemowin 'Ojibwe', or even the Attikamek 'R' dialect of Cree nêhirawêmowin). The '-win', occurring at the end of Cree and Saulteaux words, is the ending that means 'process'—all parts of the word before this describe the process.

ispimihk kâ-kitot 'sounding sky'. Sounding Sky was the father of manitowêw (Almighty Voice). The name Sounding Sky refers to the Thunderbird calling above in the sky.

manitowêw 'almighty voice'. Note the root -(a)wê for 'voice'. Almighty Voice is the legendary Cree who was arrested for killing a cow. I heard this story from nicâpânipan (my late great-grandmother), from the late Charlie Burns (yôtin 'wind'), and also from Clifford Sanderson. Interestingly, the very man who resisted government policies, had a powerful name about sound, and this sound filled the landscape with Cree being and consciousness.

têwêhikê- 'to drum'. This word is used often for traditional drumming. As best I can tell, it originally comes from Saulteaux.

môy ê-kistawêt 'it does not echo': môy or môya 'not'; ê-kistawêt 'it echoes', and -awê 'sound, voice'. I remember once when Edwin Tootoosis was visiting on James Smith Reserve at our home, my dad and uncle were loading outside, and I was asked to get Edwin tea. While getting him tea, Edwin said "môy ê-kistawêt." He asked me if I knew what that meant. I said, "Not really, môya." He then said that the earth used to be full of sound, but it does not echo today like it had kayâs 'long ago'.

cîhcêwêsin 'twisting echo'. Twisting Echo is the name of an old Cree nâpêw 'man' from my reserve nihtâwikihcikanisihk (James

Smith). Today, his family retains part of their ancestor's name in their English or anglicized name, Twist. The late Charlie Burns told me that this man had a voice like a twisting echo, a sound that cut through the air like the sound of a radio.

-htâkwan 'it makes a sound'. This cannot be used as a word by itself in Cree, but instead must be combined with an initial element that specifies how something sounds. For example, miyo- means 'good', so we can say miyohtâkwan nêhiyawêwin 'the Cree language sounds good'.

tânisi ê-isihtâkosit? 'How does s/he sound?'.

matwêhikê- 'to knock' (for example, on a door): matwê- 'to sound, be audible; be visible'; (a)h 'accomplish an action against an inanimate thing by using a tool or instrument'. Thus matwêh- is 'to make an audible knocking sound against something'. To this we can add -ikê, a useful ending that indicates there is a general action, downplaying any specific object affected by the action. This ending must always be compounded with a verb stem (like matwêh-).

• • •

Here is a wawiyatâcimowinis 'funny little story' about this word matwêhikê.

pêyakwâw ispîhk ê-mâci-kiskinohamakêyân *SIFC*îhk,
    Once, when I had just started teaching for SIFC (Saskatchewan Indian Federated College)

aya, nikî-nitaw-kiyokawâw nikâwîs ê-wîkit iskonikanihk.
I went to go visit an aunt who lived on the reserve.

ayihk,
[a word my Dad always used when he told jokes and stories]

ê-kî-osâmisîhoyân,
I was overdressed,

êkwa mîna ê-kî-cimâniskwêyân.
and I had short hair.

mitonê ê-kî-*neechie-nerd*inâkosiyân!
I truly looked like a neechie nerd.

nimatwêhikân,
I knocked on the door,

êkwa nikî-pê-paspâpamik.
and she came and looked out of the window at me. [She then returned to the inside of the house after closing the window.]

aya, kîhtwâm êkwa nikî-matwêhikân,
Well, for the second time, I knocked,

êkwa mîna, pêyakwan êkosi kî-ispayin.
and the same thing happened.

kîhtwâm nikî-pê-paspâpamik.

She came and looked out of the window at me again [and went
back into the living room, after having raised her eyebrows
ê-mâh-mahkicâpit 'with big eyes'].

âsay êkwa nistwâw nimatwêhikân,

I knocked for the third time,

êkwa mîna kinwês nikî-pê-kanawâpamik.

and she came and looked at me for a long time.

"môy nipîkiskwâtâwak *Jehovah Witnessak.*"

"I don't talk to Jehovah's Witnesses."

"wahowâ" nititwân.

"Holy smokes," I said.

"Auntie, Neal ôma!"

"Auntie, it is Neal."

"cah!" itwêw, ê-ma-mihkohkwêpayit.

"Sheesh," she said, as her face became very red.

êkwa êkwa iskwâhtêm kî-yôhtênam. nikî-piminawâtik mîciwin
mâh-mâwaci ê-wîhkasiniyik êkospîhk, môya ahpô wîpac
kîhtwâm êkotowahk nikî-mîcin.

And she opened the door. And she made me the best meal I
had that year, and for many years after.

êkosi êwako niwawiyatâcimowinis.

That was my funny little story [about the word matwêhikê].

DAY 6

PLACE NAMES (PART 1)

In the 1970s, my late mosôm, John R. McLeod, and the late John B. Tootoosis had a dream of mapping out all of Saskatchewan, using the traditional Cree terms for various places—the rivers, the dwelling places, and notable historical locations. I think it would be important to continue this work of these two Old Men, as these place names are the anchors of our collective memory.

mamâhtâwi-sîpiy This is the Cree name for the Churchill River. I would translate this name as 'the river of amazing things', 'the beautiful river that transforms the world around it'. The key element in this word is mamâhtâw, which denotes 'something beyond the ordinary; something amazing'. kistêsinaw ('Our Elder Brother') was often described as ê-mamâhtâwisit, meaning 'he does amazing things', 'he is spiritually gifted'. My uncle, the late Burton Vandall, named a computer a mamâhtâwi-âpacihcikan—'the tool that can do amazing things'. It is interesting that the word can describe both a river and a computer. There are many old paintings of powerful beings along the river, such as mêmêkwêsiwak 'the Little People' and piyêsiwak 'Thunderbirds'.

mînisihk This is the Cree name for the city of Saskatoon. It means, literally, 'at the berry'. mînis by itself means 'berry'. The -ihk ending means 'at'—for neechie nerds, this part of the word is called the locative, and it commonly marks place names.

ôtênaw Today it means a 'city', but in the old days it meant a 'camp' or '(tipi) village'. ôcênâs means a 'little town', or in kayâs ('long ago days') would mean a 'little camp'.

kistapinânihk This is the Cree name for the city of Prince Albert. This has been interpreted in a number of ways. One is 'the important resting point': kist- 'important', and sometimes you can translate this stem as 'highly'; api 'sit'; -nânihk is an extended version of that ending -ihk meaning 'at' (again, the locative). In the past, the site of the city was an important point where people would rest—it was a gathering place before the contemporary city. Many cities in Canada are located where Indigenous people lived and dwelt before.

kapêsiwin an important resting place of kistêsinaw ('Our Elder Brother'). They say he rested there one night. I have heard only fragments of this story and would love to know more, in time. This place name shows us that all of Cree territory is populated with names like this, and stories. kapêsiwin is located around Big River First Nation.

nakiwacîhk This is the Cree name for the Sweetgrass Reserve. Most reserves bear English or anglicized versions of the First Nations name of the leader who brought his people into Treaty, but there is usually another name in Cree that refers not to the leader, but to the land where the reserve is located. This name means the 'stopping hill' or 'the end of the hills': nakî- 'to stop'; waciy 'hill';

wacîhk (waciy- *plus* -ihk) is the locative form often used in place names, meaning 'at the hill(s)'. There is a glacial feature, a place where the people stopped, which marks the land and territory. It is also sometimes called the Sliding Hill.

nitahcahkomihk 'in my soul'; kitahcahkomihk 'in your soul'. An important place, the centre of our thoughts and beings, and the place from which we understand all other places.

oskana kâ-asastêki This is the Cree name for the city of Regina. It means, literally, 'pile of bones' or 'where the bones are piled': oskana 'bones'; kâ-asastêki 'where they are piled up'. This refers to both the gathering point of buffalo bones, but also marks places where our ancestors rested (their physical remains).

pâhkwâw-sâkahikan This is the Cree name for Shoal Lake ('shallow lake'), the place nicâpân Betsy McLeod (the older one), a.k.a. kêhkêhk-îskwêw ('Hawk Woman') came from. She later married my grandfather mahkiyoc ('the big one'), a.k.a. Albert McLeod.

wâskicôsihk This is the Cree name for Little Pine Reserve. wâskitoy, or the diminutive wâskicôs, refers to a 'haunch' or 'rump'. There are various explanations for the application of this name to what in English is called Blue Hill, a hill situated on the reserve. Tyrone Tootoosis Sr. suggests that, long ago, you could see from afar the white on the rumps of the elk feeding on Blue Hill. Neil Sapp, who is from Little Pine, suggests that in the landform that is Blue Hill there is what appears to be a woman lying down.

DAY 7

CLOTHING

There is a rich and detailed history of traditional Cree clothing, but in the following list are primarily contemporary clothing terms.

ayiwinisa 'clothing'. My father always talked about clothes being a very close part of our beings, and that we should be careful about our clothing.

pêyak-ayiwinis 'suit'; literally, 'the one clothing', indicating that the fabric covers the whole body. My uncle, the late Burton Vandall, used to say that word. It is funny, I live here in Ontario, and all the words he told me seem to be streaming back into the river of my mind. When he said it fast, it sounded like "pêyak-ayons" (pay-yuk eye-onz). This is an example of how the rapid speech of our people creates a rhythm that our written form of Cree does not always catch ... until you become really familiar with written Cree.

masinâstê-pêyak-ayiwinis 'zoot suit' (a striped suit).

• • •

Here is a little zoot story about my great-grandfather. My câpân often ê-kî-kikimasinâstê-pêyak-ayiwinisit ('wore a zoot suit'). He would do this especially when he would go to môniyânâhk ('white territory', a.k.a. 'town'). So I always find it strange when people say to me, "Why are you wearing a suit? Are you going to court today?" Hey, what the heck? Can't a brother be flashy in a suit of his own accord? My grandfathers all wore suits, and so do I. ahâw (cah!).

pêyakwâw nicâpân got ready to go to town. He got dressed up in his masinâstê-pêyak- ayiwinis, he put Brylcreem in his hair, and got his neechie mojo working. êkosi! He was ready to go.

He was dandied up and went to town with okosisa ('his son'). kî-takosinwak atâwêwikamikohk. They arrived at the store, looking for parts.

He walked around the store, but the môniyâwa ê-kî-atipâhpihikot 'the white people started to laugh at him', ahpô êkosi êsa itêyihtam 'or so he thought'.

Being a proud man, a man who valued his dignity, he asked my uncle (my father's brother), "Why are they laughing at me?"

"What did you put in your hair?" itwêw êsa nôhcâwîs 'my uncle said'.

"Brylcreem nikî-âpacihtân," itwêw nicâpân.

"cah! 'cha!' You have toothpaste in your hair nôhtâ!" masinâstê-pêyak-ayiwinisa can make a man, but it pays to read the labels on things when you get ready to go to town!

• • •

tâpiskâkan 'tie', also used as a word for 'collar' or even 'horse collar'.

ê-kikiskamahk 'we wear it'. My father used this phrase to describe the residential school experiences, which have become part of our beings. aya, tâpiskôc 'just like' clothing, these experiences can be taken off and new ones can be put on. Our language is part of this other clothing, which gives us strength, beauty, and dignity.

sêsâwî-ayiwinisa 'exercise clothes'.

postayiwinisê 'put on your clothes'.

kêtayiwinisê 'take off your clothes'. Certainly an interesting expression for any neechie to know. And certainly one many anthropologists would not have heard often. cah!

nôtin-astotin 'war bonnet'; literally, 'fighting hat'. The late Charlie Burns, who was kind of like my Cree Obi-Wan Kenobi, used to use this word. He used it when he told me, many times, the story of the legendary Cree leader kâ-mônahikos.

pahkêkin 'leather' (in general); ahpô cî micikos-wâyan (literally, 'the hide of the deer') means 'buckskin'.

sîwâso-kipahikana 'sunglasses'. Thanks to Dorothy Thunder for reminding me of the stem sîwâsow 's/he is affected by the glare of the sun; s/he hurts or squints from the glare of the sun'. The proposed term, then, means 'the things that block the hurt of the sun'. Dorothy came up with a better term: osîwâso-miskîsikohkâna, meaning 'the glasses that are tied to the glare of the sun'—it would be understood by context that they block that glare. kitatamihin, Dorothy, ê-kî-wîcihiyan. Thank you for your help. This is a good example of how we learn, and can learn, from those who are very skillful at Cree.

DAY 8

TREATY

The Treaties certainly play a key role in establishing the foundation for the contemporary existence of all people who dwell in the traditional homelands of the Cree people. As often has been said by the Elders of Saskatchewan, all people are Treaty people—both Indigenous people and newcomers. The Old People envisioned that through the Treaties the land could be shared among all who were involved, and that all of the descendents of the people who were party to the Treaties could live their lives with what they needed, that they could all live with dignity. To this day, the oral history of the Treaties is vividly retold and recited.

tipahamâtowin 'Treaty'; literally, 'mutual payment'. This term refers to the idea that iyinito-iyiniwak ('Indigenous people') when making the Treaties only rented the top of the land to the newcomers, to the depth of a plow, they said. If you think about it, that has huge implications for resources and so on. This runs counter to the narrative in written texts that say we "surrendered" our territories. Because of these contradictions, it is important that we hold tight to our language, words, and collective memories.

asotamâtowin 'Treaty'; specifically, 'sacred oath making'. Another way I remember my dad and the late Charlie Burns (yôtin) talking about this word is that it is a promise you have to honour no matter what—no matter how inconvenient, you have to honour it. At its core, this word gets to the upholding of honour, of being true to one's word. It also indicates a mutual responsibility.

kâ-miyikowisiyahk 'what the powers have given us'. The powers in question here are those of the land, the ancestral powers, and the Creator and all of the other beings. It is a very powerful word (really a sentence) in Cree, pointing to the core of the worldview that the Indigenous leaders would have had when they entered into Treaty.

There was an Old Man named Chipmunk (sâsâkawâpiskos) who got up at nipiy kâ-pitihkwêk in 1879 and said to Treaty Commissioner Edgar Dewdney, "How can the Queen ever replace with her promises kâ-miyikowisiyahk?" I have thought about the Old Man's words for a long time, and I think that he was thinking ahead for his people, the nêhiyawak 'Cree', and also the nahkawiyiniwak 'Saulteaux' and pwâsîmowak 'Assiniboine Nakota'. He thought about what the Queen was offering and knew that the nêhiyawak already had what we needed.

cowêhikanâpisîs 'Dragonfly'. Old Man French Eater from wâskicôsihk (Little Pine Reserve) designated cowêhikanâpisîs as a Métis interpreter. He noted that cowêhikanâpisîs spoke very good Cree. Since Old Man French Eater was from wâskicôsihk, I think it would be reasonable to hypothesize cowêhikanâpisîs was at nipiy kâ-pitihkwêk in 1879, which was a major Treaty Adhesion.

itâskonikê- 'to have a pipe ceremony', 'to invoke the pipe and prayers'. This ceremony was central to the process of Treaty-making for the nêhiyawak.

oskiciy 'pipestem'.

pêhonânihk Fort Carlton; literally, 'at the Waiting Place'. A major place of gathering where Treaty Six was entered into. It was also a key fur trading post where many of my ancestors (of the wâskahikaniwiyiniwak 'the House People') traded. pêho means 'wait'.

wâskahikanis Fort Pitt; literally, 'little house' or 'little fort'. This was another place where Treaty Six was entered into. Many of the sîpîwiyiniwak 'River People' entered there. The old kayâs ago nêhiyawak (Crees) called fur trading posts wâskahikana, a term we often use to mean 'houses' today.

wiyihcikê- 'to make a Treaty'. The word can also be used to mean 'negotiations'.

miyo-wîcihitowin 'to share things well together'. One of the central philosophical pillars of how our ancestors understood the Treaty process, mutual aid, and responsibility. The Woods Cree word for this is mitho-wîcihitowin.

kiskinowâpisk 'Treaty medal'; literally, 'the metal which guides'. I think this could refer to the picture on the medal—in which the First Nations man shakes hands with the European newcomer. Perhaps one could think of miyo-wîcihitowin as embedded in this word or concept. It was one of the last words the late Charlie Burns (yôtin) taught me.

kâ-kî-pê-pimohtêstamawât kihc-ôkimâskwêwa 'Treaty Commissioner'; literally, 'the one who walks for the Queen'. The expression comes from the late Jim Kâ-Nîpitêhtêw. ana kisêyinîpan ê-kî-tâpâhkômât nimosômipana 'This late Old Man adopted my late mosôm' (John R. McLeod). They worked together on Treaty issues, stories, and "honourings" (I know that word is made up in English, but I like it).

DAY 9

FACEBOOK/
INTERNET SLANG

All too often people think that technology and television are negative factors leading to the decline of Indigenous languages, including Cree. However, I would say the Internet, including Facebook, is a tool that can help with language retention. Social media played a key role in the writing of this book. Words were posted, and then people from all over Canada and the United States contributed to our ongoing quest to document the Cree language.

*facebook*ipitamawin 'facebook me!'.

ê-wî-*post*opitamân anima 'I will post that'.

ni*wall*im 'my wall'.

mihkwâkan-masinahikan 'Facebook'. In Anishinaabemowin: ndengwajgan mzinaganishin. Remember, our Anishaabeg brothers and sisters, you are the wind beneath our Cree wings.

ayapîhkêsîs isi-pîkiskwêwin 'words from the Internet/World Wide Web'; literally, 'the language of spiders'. I remember hearing this years ago, or reading it on an art-event poster.

mosci-pîkiskwêwin 'chat'; literally, 'just merely speaking' (or something to that effect). The particle mosci- is a tricky little bundle of sound; be careful not to mix it up with môhco- 'foolish'! I remember once, someone said to me, "Neal, ê-mosci-nâpêwiyan." I though it meant, "Neal, it is as though you are a man—you are kêkâc 'almost' a man, but not quite." Maybe I was just being called a crazy man, or maybe I was told that I was just a man, no more and no less.

ê-kakwê-nôcihiskwêwêyan cî *Facebook*-askîhk? 'Are you trying to score on Facebook?'. If your game is nâpêwak 'men', then you could change this to ê-kakwê-nôcinâpêwêyan cî *Facebook*-askîhk. "It does not matter what your game is, as long as you have game."

sêwêpicikanis icwêwinisa 'text'; literally, 'the little telephone words'. This word came from Tessa Desnomie and kihci Billy "The Kid" Cook, and their Woodland or Rock Cree version would be sîwîpicikanis icwîwinisa. To find the heart of Cree and understand the words, you must break down all of the stems. I remember my dad used to speak of an Old Man from Whitefish who had very descriptive words and language. All of the words are like little poems, and you have to try and figure out the stems and meanings. My dad said when that Old Man would speak, he could close his eyes and the words would become pictures in his mind.

The first stem of this expression is sêwêpicikê- 'to make a ringing sound'. Altering the ending to -kan changes the bannock mix of this word, êkwa mîna you have sêwêpicikan (sîwîpicikan in Woodland Cree) 'ringing device'. One more little spice is the -is at the end, which just makes it 'the little thing being described'. So the word for cell phone is like 'the little thing that rings'. I guess if you had it on vibrate, you could call it nanamipayihcikanis, literally, the 'little thing that vibrates'. If it is in your pants, quit getting your friends to keep phoning you over and over again. cah!

Now this word sêwêpicikanis needs a side dish, another word, icwêwinisa, which means 'little words, little sayings'. itwê- is the verb stem for 'say it', and then adding -win makes it a process or thing. Thus, itwêwin means 'word' or 'saying' (it is really referring to a spoken word, a 'saying'—not a text or written word). In order to indicate that we're talking about little words (that is, to apisîs-size it), we add the ending -is again. But in itwêwin we also have a /t/, which changes to a [c]: icwêwinis. Whenever you want to make something into a 'little something' and there is a /t/ in the word, you change the /t/ to a [c]. For instance, if you were talking to a baby as you rocked him or her, you would say "câpwê! câpwê!" (tâpwê! tâpwê!). At the very end of this word you have -a, which tells you there is more than one little word: icwêwinisa ('little words').

konita-tôtêm 'Facebook friend who you really have no real connection with'. konita really means 'for no purpose'.

cah! Don't say "jks"—be a neechie and say cah! (pronounced "cha!"). Assimilation starts in small little steps, and this is one of them. If we are to survive, we must draw the line here. We must bring back the cah!

DAY 10

HORSES (PART 1)

For the nêhiyawak (Plains Cree), mistatimwak 'horses' were at the core of social, cultural, and spiritual beliefs. Our stories are full of references to and imagery of mistatimwak. Singular mistatim literally means 'big dog'. Some dialects use misatim and misatimwak.

mihkominis sâkahikan 'Red Berry Lake'. This is a very special and beautiful lake between Saskatoon and North Battleford (at roughly the halfway point between the two cities on the Yellowhead Highway). nicâpân used to speak of this lake and how horses would come out of the water there. Sometimes, my father told me, nêhiyawak would bring their horses to this place to mate with the beautiful, powerful horses that would emerge there.

kâ-ocipicikêsicik mistatimwak 'pulling horses'. This maskêko-Cree word is courtesy of Chris Hunter. (Thanks for always answering my questions, nitôtêm. kinanâskomitin.) Whoever has Chris for a Cree teacher is very lucky—I always learn from him. He gave me this word when I asked him to describe a team of horses.

sâkocih 'overcome', 'win someone over'. This word is, once again, courtesy of Chris Hunter. I asked him how you would say "break a horse." This is the word his family used for training dogs, and it suggests a very different philosophical concept than breaking a horse. Instead of "breaking" when training, you "try to convince them, to win them over," as Chris Hunter says. "You have to earn their trust," itwêw Chris. His parents used that term a lot because they had dog sleds in their backyard, and they were experts in sled-dog training. In some dialects of Plains Cree, this word means 'to dominate or overwhelm'. But I remember hearing a story where the use and meaning of sâkocih meant more to 'convince' someone (and the form sâkocim specifically means 'to convince someone or win someone over verbally'). It is interesting to note the changes that words may have undergone from maskêko-Cree to Plains Cree. Also, it is interesting to note that at one time our main animals for moving things were atimwak 'dogs'. Then, as Crees, we relied more on mistatimwak and moved more and more onto the Plains. Women owned the dogs, and men owned the horses (generally). I am becoming more and more convinced that to understand the Plains Cree dialect, we have to explore the layers and history of the meanings of these words. Studying maskêko-Cree is essential to this research.

nakayâhastimwê- 'to break a horse' (Plains Cree).

mistatimahpicikana 'horse reins'; literally, 'horse belts'.

wiyahpicikana alternative for 'horse reins'.

têhtapi- 'to ride [a horse]'.

têhtapiwatim 'saddle horse'.

kotiskâwêw mistatim *or* **kotiskâwêwatim** 'thoroughbred horse'; literally, 'racing horse'. Used to denote horses at the race track in contemporary times.

mistatim ê-aspinît 'horse snort'.

aspapiwin 'saddle'.

nitâhtâm mistatim 'borrow a horse'! From the kayâs ago days of warfare.

miywatim 'a beautiful horse'. Note that sometimes when compounding (putting stems together in Cree), the stem atim 'dog' is often used as a shortened form to refer to horses. This word is an example of that, and it can also mean 'good dog'. Sometimes, another variant, -astim, is used, and this can also refer to dogs or horses, as in the next example.

nôsêstim 'a mare'. There are two roots that are combining here: nôsê-, referring to a 'female' or 'female animal', is combined with -astim (a variant of atim, which is sometimes used in compounding). The vowel from the first stem overlaps the vowel of the second stem. Linguists call this "elision."

masinâsowatim 'painted horse'.

misatimosimowin 'horse dance'. I have been blessed to hear some powerful songs from this ceremony.

•••

After working on this list, I realized that we need to gather the specialized vocabulary of various elements of our language. Facebook was helpful with this task—despite its limitations. I found that if we could focus on a word/theme, then we could try to think of related vocabulary. Also, as I dug deeper into our language, I realized, as my friend Jerry Fineday once said, mitoni wêyôtan ôma 'it is truly deep', our language.

Here is some interesting horse imagery from my late câpân 'great-grandfather' Peter Vandall from yêkawiskâwikamâhk (Sandy Lake, Saskatchewan), as recorded on pages 46–47 in *wâskahikaniwiyiniw-âcimowina/Stories of the House People*, edited and translated by Freda Ahenakew (University of Manitoba Press, 1987). omisi kî-itwêw:

êkwa mâna namôya kakêtihk misâhkamik, kî-âtotamwak, kêhtê-ayak, tâpiskôc akâmôtênaw mitoni têpiyâhk ê-wâpamat misatim aya, ê-wâpiskisit, iyikohk ê-misi-wîhkwêstêki mâna mîkiwâhpa ôhi, iyikohk ê-kî-itêyatit nêhiyaw kayâs.

'And there were great numbers of people, the elders used to tell, across the camp-circle, for instance, one could barely distinguish a horse even if it was white, so big was the circle of these tipis, there were so many Crees long ago'.

DIFFERENT PEOPLES

One of the key clusters of words in Cree is the names of various nations. These names give us the threads to conceptually understand the history that surrounded the Cree people, and also gives the history of the Crees' form and embodiment. Knowing the names of various nations gives us access to narratives of Cree history, which in turn allow us to understand the past from the perspective of Cree people. The names of various nations give us narrative threads of memory and consciousness, and they are entry points to pathways of eternity.

nêhiyawak 'the Crees', particularly the Plains Cree or 'y' dialect. nîhithawak means 'Woodlands Cree', 'th' dialect; and ininiwak or maskêkowininiwak means 'Swampy or maskêko-Cree', 'n' dialect.

nêhiyawi-pwâtak 'the Cree-Sioux' or 'Assiniboine-Cree'. They were known back in the kayâs ago days also as the 'Young Dogs'. The descendants of these people are the people of Piapot [payipwât] First Nation. The late Beatrice Lavallee, a dearly beloved kôhkom, told me that they had deep kinship ties with the Assiniboine people at Carry the Kettle. Back in the kayâs ago days, they would meet each other and have ceremonies together. In recent times, these old ties have been rethreaded and tied back together.

asinîwipwâtak 'the Assiniboine' (or Nakota); literally, the 'Stone' Siouan people (sorry for the anthropological twang). pwâtak on its own means 'Dakota'. The asinîwipwâtak have been allies with the nêhiyawak for hundreds of years. Once, when I asked my dad why they were called the Stone Siouan people, he said it was because they used to cook by using warm stones placed in the stomachs of animals.

pwâsîmowak 'the Assiniboine' (or sometimes called 'Stonies'). Around the Battlefords area, this term has often been used. pwâsîmo means 'speak Assiniboine'.

wâskitôwiyiniwak *or* **wâskicôsiyiniwak** This is the term that Neil Sapp gave me for the people of Little Pine. The word is a reference, by metaphor, to the Blue Hill, which was a grazing place, a hill that they say looked like a woman's body. (*See* Day 6.)

kâ-kaskitêsîhocik 'those who dress in black'. This is the term for neechie Johnny Cash interpreters. Just kidding! I have heard this term a few times in reference to Hutterites, because they dress in black.

mâyacihkwayâniyiniwak 'Russians'; literally, 'sheep hide people'. I heard this term years ago at wîhcêkaskosiy-sâkahikan (Onion Lake), when I first started teaching for Saskatchewan Indian Federated College, back in the kayâs ago days. Apparently, this describes the garb worn by some of the Russians that some nêhiyawak encountered.

sêkipacwâs 'Chinese'; as I heard it described, this word refers to the Chinese style of having one braid. I wonder if old school neechies ever had braid envy. cah!

ayahciyiniwak 'Blackfoot', but literally, 'strangers', a word also applied to the Slavey and possibly other groups. In the Cree Bible, the term ayahciyiniwak is used for 'Gentiles'. Was nêhiyawak used for Gentiles in Blackfoot translations? cah!

sâsîwak 'Sarcee'. A group that was part of the Blackfoot Confederacy. They were really Dene (or Athapaskan) people that came south in the mid-1700s to join the Blackfoot. They live west of Calgary and today call themselves Tsuu T'ina.

kâ-têpwêwi-sîpîwiyiniwak 'the Calling River People'. This refers to the Cree and Saulteaux people of the Qu'Appelle Valley. David Mandelbaum (in *The Plains Cree*) mistakenly says the people in this area are only Plains Cree, but, in fact, they have a strong Saulteaux element.

nakawiyiniwak 'Saulteaux'. I understand this term to come from the Saulteaux practice of clipping their words, so, from a Cree perspective, they were the ones who 'ended their words'. I stand to be corrected, of course.

wêmistikôsiwak 'French people'. That is the meaning of this term from my reserve, James Smith. There was a man at the time of Treaty who signed the Treaty with the word cikos, a radically abbreviated version of this name (really meaning 'the little French Man'). Literally, the word means 'the people of the wooden boats': mistik 'wooden'; ôsi 'canoe' or 'boat'.

âpihtawikosisânak 'Métis'. I know that some people do not like this term because it means 'half-son'. The obvious question is, *what about the daughters?* And also why would Métis people be described as only being 'half' and not whole beings? Just food for thought. I heard another term once when my dad and I were visiting Edwin Tootoosis on Poundmaker Reserve. My dad referred to one of our relatives who spoke Cree, but didn't have status, as êkâ ê-akimiht (literally, 'the one who is not counted'). The term is in present tense and also notes, subtley, the practical way in which nêhiyawak and Métis were related to each other, that the boundary between the two is often very arbitrary.

THE CHARACTER AND KNOWLEDGE OF THE CREES

FROM *PLAINS CREE TEXTS*

The following terms come from stories collected by Leonard Bloomfield on the Sweetgrass Reserve (nakiwacîhk) in the 1920s. These narratives were collected at the height of repression of Indigenous ceremonies, which, I think, shows the tensions within colonial consciousness. The narrator was Louis Moosomin.

These stories are important because they provide us with profound and deep resources in our language, giving us a way to learn terms in the context of other words and ideas in which those terms were spoken. We need more books like Bloomfield's from which to draw the great wisdom of our collective memory. These types of narratives provide us with sources to understand the honour of our ancestors.

wêyôtisiwin 'wealth', connoting European wealth. It has to be remembered that these texts were gathered in the 1920s, and the narrators were living through poverty and severe repression, both culturally and politically.

k-ôh-kitimâkisiyahk 'the reason why we are poor': k-ôh- is reduced from kâ-ohci- 'from which' (ohci- 'from'); kitimâkisi- is the verb stem 'to be pitiful and/or poor'. I think that if this text was to be retranslated, the aspect of 'being pitiful' should be embedded in the new translation of this sentence.

ayâw nêhiyaw kisêwâtisiwin 'the Cree has kindness': ayâ- 'to have, to be'; nêhiyaw 'Cree'; kisêwâtisiwin 'kindness'. I have heard that kisêyiniw really means 'kind man': kisê- 'kind'; iyiniw 'person' or 'man'. It is interesting that despite the extreme pressures put upon the Cree people at this time, the Old Man, Louis Moosomin, still stressed kindness.

wîci-ayisiyinîma 'his/her fellow person' (note that in Cree this is not gendered per se). The -a ending on -ayisiyinîm- shows that it is in the obviative form (or fourth-person form, in deference to the one related to, that is, 'his/her'). The narrator goes on to say how we would share with one another and have empathy for one another.

kâ-kî-isi-pakitiniht 'that which [the Cree] was set down here on earth' or 'how [the Cree] was provided for'. kâ- here means 'that which is'. The rest of the sentence then describes kâ-. Many names begin with kâ-: it can mean 'the one who'. kî- is the past-tense marker; isi- suggests the manner in which something is done (for example, tânisi 'how' has the element of -isi in it); pakitin- means 'to allow, permit', and in this sense 'to provide'; and the ending -iht indicates that the giver is not mentioned or named (though perhaps is implied as the Creator).

pîwâpisk ohci mâna ayisiyiniwa The whole phrase is translated as 'men who were made of metal': pîwâpisk 'iron'; ê-osîhâcik 'they make them' (described in the rest of the sentence as 'out of metal'). The description of metal may have references to the fur trade, but perhaps only indirectly. (Note: Bloomfield marked a lot of words that should end in vowels with an 'h' aspiration at the end; for example, in the original text where this phrase appears, he wrote mânah, which is now standardly written as mâna.)

ê-manitôwit 'he had spirit power'.

pîhtokê 'enter'. Note that in contemporary Cree, variants like pîhtokwê and pîhtikwê are heard in some dialects.

aswêyim- 'to be on the look out [against someone]'.

nâh-namiskwêkâpaw This was Louis Moosomin's name in Cree. namiskwê- means 'to nod one's head' and -kâpaw(i) means 'to stand', while nâh- at the beginning reduplicates the verb (indicating repeated action). So his name was loosely: 'he stands nodding his head' or 'he stands bowing'.

DAY 13

KINSHIP

Those of you who are academics use wâhkôhtowin as a core interpretative concept when writing methodology papers. We don't always have to interpret our being and consciousness through the interpretative and linguistic lens of English. wâhkôhtowin is what links us and what binds us all together through time across generations. It should be noted that wâhkôhtowin exists not only between people but also between all parts of creation.

wâhkôhtowin 'kinship', the way in which we are related to each other.

wâhkôm- 'to be related [to someone]'.

niwâhkômâkanak 'my relatives'.

niwâhkômâkanitik 'My Relatives!'. The -itik ending makes it a more formal means of address; neechie nerds like me call this the "vocative." It would be used only when the speaker (that is, the "first person") is addressing others. My father, when he spoke, often used -tik at the end of verbs for 'they' (third person plural). I am wondering if that is remnant of a more classical verb structure. Now it is –cik, which could theoretically be viewed as a diminutive -itik; however, the change of /t/ to [c] occurs elsewhere in the language, as well. (Note to neechie nerds: this sound change is called "palatalization.")

nitôtêm 'my friend'. Interesting that, in Anishinaabemowin, the word for 'clan' is doodem and this was the word taken into English as 'totem'. It seems that Cree has "secularized" this more ancient meaning in Anishinaabemowin. However, some still use -tôtêm to refer to a fellow member of one's band.

tâpâhkôm- 'to adopt [someone]'. I think of two examples here: I think of the Grandfather Buffalo who adopted paskwâ-mostos awâsis ('Buffalo Child'); I also think of the late Jim Kâ-Nîpitêhtêw (kâ-pimwêwêhahk) who adopted nimosômipan (my late mosôm) John R. McLeod. The latter two worked together extensively in the commemoration of Treaty Six in 1976.

nôhkom 'my grandmother'.

nimosôm 'my grandfather'.

nicâpân 'my great-grandfather' or 'my great-grandmother'. If I am not mistaken, this word is rooted in the stem –tâpân, which means 'to carry something along' (for example: otâpânask 'vehicle'). Poetically, our great-grandparents are described as 'those who carry things'. This term is also used to describe a 'great-grandchild', who, by extension, would carry things in the future (for example, the cultural and linguistic legacy of our people).

nistês 'my older brother'. It is interesting that the nêhiyawak would, a long time ago, and even today to some extent, consider it rude to address people by their first names. Rather, they want(ed) to address people through some kinship term. Thus, another way to refer to wîsahkêcâhk (Trickster) is kistêsinaw 'our older brother'. As far as I can tell, the term "Trickster" is an English invention.

nimis 'my older sister'.

nisîmis 'my younger sibling'.

nikâwiy 'my mother'. Many have replaced this with nimâmâ. Sometimes, when addressing one's mother, an older, vocative singular form is still used: nikâ or nêkâ 'Mom!'.

nôhtâwiy 'my father'. Many have replaced this with nipâpâ. Sometimes, when addressing one's father, an older, vocative singular form is still used: nôhtâ 'Dad!'.

nôhcâwîs 'my dear father' ('my uncle'; 'my father's brother', 'my mother's sister's husband').

nîkâwîs 'my dear mother' ('my aunt'; 'my mother's sister', 'my father's brother's wife').

nîtim This literally means 'my cross-cousin of the opposite gender', which is obviously a concept and kinship relationship that English has a lot of trouble expressing. A man uses nîtim to refer to his father's sister's daughter or mother's brother's daughter (that is, his female cross-cousin), and a woman uses nîtim to refer to her father's sister's son or mother's brother's son (that is, her male cross-cousin). In the traditional kinship system, your parallel cousins (father's brother's children and mother's sister's children) were just like your own siblings, but cross-cousins were considered more distinctly and distantly related. Parallel cousins and siblings could not marry, but cross-cousins could marry if no other potential partners were available. So, the term nîtim is used reciprocally by men and women who are related but may still be potential partners. The diminutive or endearing form, nîcimos, thus indicates that the potential relationship has gone beyond potential, and thus leads to the translation 'sweetheart'. Today, this term is used for 'boyfriend' and 'girlfriend'.

nitiskwêm 'the woman who is very close to me'. Grammatical note: the -im ending added to some nouns (like iskwêw 'woman' becoming -iskwêm) indicates that there is a special relationship involved.

ninâpêm 'the man who is very close to me'. As above, nâpêw 'man' becomes -nâpêm.

nimanâcimâkan 'my respected one'. This is a classical Cree term used for a special relationship between either a father-in-law and his daughter-in-law (that is, a man and his son's wife) or a mother-in-law and her son-in-law (that is, a woman and her daughter's husband). It really means 'the one I respect' and was often marked by strict avoidance protocols (once again, evidence that our philosophy rests in our language and not in intellectual shell games).

DANCES
FROM *PLAINS CREE TEXTS*

The terms below come from stories collected by Leonard Bloomfield on the Sweetgrass Reserve (nakiwacîhk) in the 1920s. The narrator Bloomfield recorded in this instance was sâkêwêw (Adam Sâkêwêw). The artist collective in which I was very active in the late 1990s and early 2000s bears the same name: Sâkêwêwak 'they come into view', 'they emerge'. The root sâk- means to 'emerge, protrude'. Another word with this root is ê-pê-sâkâstêk 'the coming dawn': literally, pê- 'come' *plus* sâk- combined with the stem -âstê- 'light; shine', meaning 'the emergence of light'. Once again we see that Cree is a very profoundly poetic language. Our close relatives, the Saulteaux, of course, also have this deeply poetic, sonoric rhythm in their names and words.

The narrative from which these terms are derived talks a lot about nipâkwêsimowin (the Thirst Dance). Of course, the appropriate place to talk about these matters is in the company of kêhtê-ayak. However, I want to focus on some of the words and vocabulary and philosophy within these narratives, and as such I have chosen the following phrases.

kahkiyaw ayisiyiniw kita-ohpikit ôta askîhk 'all people will grow into their being on this earth' (my proposed interpretation of this line). While I admire and respect Bloomfield's work, I think that another interpretation of this precious text is worthwhile. Within this text is a great narrative legacy. kahkiyaw 'all'; ayisiyiniw 'person'; kita-ohpikit 'will grow into their being'; ôta 'here'; askiy 'earth' (but 'on this earth' is askîhk; the -(i)hk part of the word is called a locative, denoting place).

sêmâk kahkiyaw kîwâniwiw, ê-nitawi-atoskêhk 'immediately everyone goes home, and engages in work': sêmâk 'immediately'; kîwê 'to go home' (kîwâniwiw is an 'unspecified actor' or generic form of the verb); nitawi- 'to go do something' (completed by a verb stem that has to follow grammatically); atoskê 'work'.

Once again, it must be remembered that the narratives in *Plains Cree Texts* were recorded at the height of the repression of Indigenous ceremonies on the prairies. Government officials like William Graham (kâ-mistikokât 'Wooden Leg') thought that our ceremonies took away from our work. Thus, the narrator, knowing that the book provides him with access to a large audience, notes that the people, after honouring creation through the ceremony, will work hard. It is unfortunate that government officials did not see the hardworking nature of nêhiyawak. I, for one, learned an intense work ethic and drive from my father, who learned this from his parents and grandparents.

namôya wîhkâc ê-kisiwâsihk... 'Never in anger....'. Note that today, namôya is often pronounced môy in rapid speech. I have in my possession a syllabics Bible from my câpân, kêhkêhk-iskwêw ('Hawk Woman'), and in this Bible, namôya is rendered as namawiya.

This shows that even our full form namôya is contracted from a yet older, longer form.

...êwako mîkiwâhp k-âpacihtâcik nêhiyawak '...would the Cree use this lodge [in the manner described above]' (sentence continued from previous entry). êwako is an interesting flavouring word in Cree—kind of like one of the Colonel's spices. It refers to something that has been previously mentioned or which is understood from the context of the story. mîkiwâhp 'tipi' is used here to refer to the Thirst Dance Lodge (note: tipi is an Assiniboine [Stoney/Nakota] and Dakota [Sioux] word for 'living place'); âpacihtâ 'to use'; nêhiyawak 'Crees'.

mistahi mihcêtwâw ohci-pimâtisiwak nêhiyawak 'Truly a large number of Crees received life [from this]' (that is, from the lodge): mistahi 'lots, a great amount' (for example, mistahi-maskwa: the name of this great Cree leader literally means 'a lot of Bear'); mihcêtwâw 'many times'; ohci 'from' (for example, tânitê ohci kiya? 'where do you come from?'); pimâtisi 'to live, to have life' (not to be confused with wîki-, the verb stem that means 'to live someplace, to dwell, to reside').

ê-âhkosit awiyak, asotam 'when one is sick, one makes a vow': âhkosi 'to be sick'; asota 'to make a vow'. I am quite struck by this phrase and the use of this verb here. The verb stem asota is the same stem that is in one of the Cree words for Treaty making, asotamâtowin. (See Day 8.) The first verbs that those learning Cree encounter are in the conjunct mode, which means they are part of a dependent clause, and the main verb/clause will follow. However, please note that in some dialects, in conversational speech, people use the conjunct mode extensively in general.

miy sôhkisiwin 'give him strength, tenacity' (my translation). Bloomfield translates the noun sôhkisiwin as 'moderation', but, with all due respect to him, I think he is off a bit here. sâkêwêw goes on to describe the use of tobacco and the relationship to a child that is described in the story, and also who they are praying for: kâ-kanawêyihtamawak cistêmâwa 'the one for whom I am taking care of the tobacco'. This sentence still needs a bit of work, but it is a beautiful sentence, as is the idea behind it. It is also an interesting expression of traditional protocol.

For those who are academics, I would encourage you to explore the discussion of terms like miy sôhkisiwin in Cree, rather than simply talking about Indigenous Knowledge in English. To be meaningful, Indigenous Knowledge has to be grounded in our language, and from the language come our concepts and thinking. I mean no disrespect in giving this gentle reminder.

kisêwâtisiwak 'they are kind'. Here sâkêwêw is talking about the Beings who are involved in the Thirst Dance ceremony. Once again, the narrator, like Louis Moosomin, stresses kindness. I am again struck by the patience and intelligence our Old People had during this time of great turmoil and challenge.

kitimâkihtawin 'have pity on me', 'hear me in pity'. This is a common expression in Cree prayers.

êwako kahkiyaw a more classical and elegant way of saying êkosi 'that is it, that is all'.

kahkiyaw êkosi a slight variation of the above.

• • •

mêtoni tâpwê wêyôtan kêhtê-ayak kâ-kî-nakatamâkoyahkik,
ê-pakaski-nêhiyawêcik ê-âcimocik ôta masinahikanihk 'Truly
what the Old Ones have left us in these stories in this book is
rich and deep'. (And high Cree!) mâh-mâmitonêyihtamahki ôhi,
kika-ati-mâci-nisitohtênaw nêhiyawi-mâmitonêyihcikan 'Through
thinking through these, we will begin to understand Cree consciousness'.

DAY 15

MEDICINE

I don't want to break any protocols by talking about medicines, but I think that I can respectfully mention some things here about plants and medicines. At least this might spark someone's interest and prompt them to sit with kêhtê-ayak and learn directly.

One of my grandmothers, cîhcam, who died in 1966, was a well-known healer. She was the daughter of masaskâpaw (Masuskapoe), and through her actions of gathering medicines was able to maintain the connection to land and territory. That she was the anchor of my family demonstrates the strength of women. More research could be done on the displacement of Indigenous women from helping people with their health and spiritual needs, and the place of Indigenous women generally within society, particularly in western Canada.

maskihkiy 'medicine'.

nêhiyawi-maskihkiy 'Cree medicine'.

mêmêkwêsiwak 'the Little People' (also, apisciyinîsak). There are stories about people who have dreams and go through doorways of trees, and meet the mêmêkwêsiwak. The mêmêkwêsiwak would then give the dreamer plants and medicines after being presented with ribbon, tobacco, and cloth. I learned all of this from Old People from the James Smith Reserve.

nâcinêhamaw 'to give an offering for medicine', 'to obtain medicine'.

-ask(w) 'medicine'; literally, 'plant'. This root (if you'll forgive the linguistic pun) occurs at the end of words; the stem placed in front of this describes the type of medicine.

mînisîhkês 'Seneca root'. Many Indigenous women used to gather this root and sell it to newcomers for extra income. Of course, this root was also an important medicine used by our own people.

wîhkês A bitter-tasting medicine that looks like ginger root. It is used as a tea or chewed. The word is wînkês in Saulteaux, and it is often translated as 'rat-root', in reference to the muskrat.

kâ-mistanâskowêw 'Calling Badger' or 'Badger Voice', the man gifted with syllabics by the Creator. He was originally from Stanley Mission in present-day Saskatchewan, and later moved to the Battlefords area. When the Creator gave kâ-mistanâskowêw syllabics, the Creator compared the writing to maskihkiy.

miyâhkas- 'to smudge something'.

miyâhkasikê- 'to smudge'.

miyâhkas(w)- 'to smudge [someone]'. When the suppression of our ceremonies was at its peak in the 1920s and the 1930s, many of our kêhtê-ayak would smudge people under tables and doctor them in secret to avoid detection by government officials. My câpân, cîhcam, the daughter of masaskâpaw and niece of atâhk-akohp, used to do this.

PLACE NAMES (PART 2)

I wanted to follow up with another list of Cree place names because they are like bundles of stories that give us access to the lived experiences and stories of those who walked and lived on the land before us.

If there were Cree place names on road signs and maps, there would be a great philosophical shift in thinking in western Canada. The signs would remind people of old stories and of the old Cree presence in this territory. It would also instill within young Indigenous people a pride and reminder of their ancestral dignity, which they could take into the present.

paskwâwi-sâkahikan 'Meadow Lake'. paskwâw is the stem for 'there is prairie, plains' or 'there is a clearing'—but the original Cree image here is that 'it is bald land'. In paskwâwi-, the -i is added to the stem to make it an adjectival or a descriptive element used in compounding. So, literally, it means 'the lake of the clearing'. In Saulteaux, it is paškwâ (š = 'sh').

maskihkiy-astôtin 'Medicine Hat'. Many times, the late Charlie Burns told me the story of kâ-monakos (kâ-mônahikos; I just like to write it the way I heard Charlie say it because it reminds me of him). He heard it from his mosôm côcam 'the one who does little things', who in turn heard it from iskotêw 'Fire', who was the original 'Burns'. There is a long story of how the Cree were surrounded by the Blackfoot where the city of Medicine Hat is now located. A Blackfoot wanted to marry kâ-mônahikos's daughter. In exchange, the Blackfoot said they would leave the Cree alone. kâ-mônahikos said, "môya," and he threw his nôtinastotin 'war bonnet' in the river.

mikisiwacîhk 'at the Eagle Hills': mikisiw 'eagle'; waciy 'hill(s)' *plus* the locative -ihk. This is an important place for the River People. It also refers to the land mass of Red Pheasant First Nation. Notice that most reserves have at least two names: one name is for the leader at or around the time of Treaty, and the other one is a description of the land.

sâkitawâhk 'North Battleford' (probably also refers to 'the Battlefords'; and, if I am not mistaken, sâkitawâhk also refers to Île-à-la-Crosse). The name refers to the mouth of a river, where waters meet. Remember that the root sâk- means 'to protrude', 'to stick out'.

nôtinitowi-sîpiy 'Battle River'. This was the traditional marker of the border between the nêhiyawak and the ayahciyiniwak 'the Blackfoot'.

amiskwaciy-wâskahikan 'Beaver Hills House', which is Edmonton. This was the main fort for the amiskwacîwiyiniwak 'the Beaver Hills People'. In the Day 8 entries (about Treaty), I commented on the use of wâskahikan for 'house', but this term was originally used for the trading fort.

kisiskâciwani-sîpiy Saskatchewan River, namely, 'the fast-flowing River': kisiskâ- 'fast' -ciwan, 'to flow'. This has been anglicized to 'Saskatchewan'. How does the kisiskâciwan Roughriders sound? Or Hotel kisiskâciwan?

pâwistikowiyiniw-sîpiy Refers to part of the South Saskatchewan River in the vicinity of Batoche. pâwistikowiyiniw refers to the 'Rapids People' (also known as the 'White Clay People', the Gros Ventres or Atsina). They are culturally close to the Arapaho, and at times occupied large parts of what is today Saskatchewan. They were in a bitter fight with the Crees for part of the 1800s.

mistahi-sâkahikan Lac La Ronge, Saskatchewan; literally, 'Big Lake' or 'lots of lake'.

DAY 17

WARFARE

I have always had a great interest in Cree warfare. My book of poems called *Gabriel's Beach* examined the old concepts of warfare, as well as ideas of Indigenous masculinity. Much of our understanding of these ideas has been lost, and I believe the retrieval of these stories would help our young people a great deal. It was in warfare that Indigenous men could, at least in part, demonstrate honour in their lives.

onitowatâw 'scout'. This term is courtesy of Wes Fineday, and I remember that he also once referred to artists as 'scouts'.

nitâhtâmo-mistatim 'borrowed horse'. In the old system of warfare, to 'borrow' a horse was a sign of honour and courage.

ê-misoht 'he is wounded'. To quote Wes Fineday, this term is "from the old form of the language." To keep the classical depth of nêhiyawêwin, we need as many of these terms as possible.

nôtinastotin 'war bonnet'; literally, 'war hat'. The late Charlie Burns taught me this term when he told me the story of maskihkiy-astotin.

ê-nêhiyawatâmot 'to sing your special song/power song'. Charlie Burns taught me this term as well. Some people have called this a death song, but it is more than that. It is the song that people got their power from. He told me this word when he would recite the story of kâ-manitowêw 'Almighty Voice'.

ahcâpiy 'bow'.

atos 'arrow'.

pîhtatwân 'quiver'.

nahâskwêw 's/he has a good shot'. The -âskw- root in the middle of this word refers to the wood of the arrow, part of the weaponry of the okihcitâwak of yesteryear. As is common in Cree, the original understanding of the term has been extended to contemporary warfare and snipers. This term was used in the First and Second World Wars. The term kâ-nahâskwêt means 'sniper'. Remember, kâ- is put in front of verbs, and in front of names, and means something like 'the one who...'; then the verb comes in to describe what the person is. I heard both my father and Wes Fineday use this word.

pimotâhkwêw another word for 'a good shot'. Note: -âhkw- is a variant of -âskw-.

kihci-âcimowina 'the stories of warfare' (often between the nêhiyawak 'Crees' and ayahciyiniwak 'Blackfoot'). As told to me by my friend Ray Cardinal, in parts of Alberta the term ayahciyiniwak refers to the Slavey Indigenous Nation. The term kihci-âcimowina really means 'the highest stories'. It should not be surprising that Cree men would use this term for warfare. I wonder what we would call kihci-âcimowina today. Something to consider.

DAY 18

RIVERS

The rivers were our highways in the old days, and the source of so much life and many gifts. In Treaty Six, the flow of rivers was one of the things by which the old Crees made a pledge—the classic line: "as long as the rivers flow." The rivers flowed, and wound through the territory, and gave people life. I think it is noteworthy today that the Anishinaabeg have water walks to honour the power and gifts of the water.

sîpiy 'river'.

sîpîsis 'little river; creek'. Adding -(is)is to words indicates a smaller form of the original stem (that is, the diminutive). I remember my dad used to joke and call me "'Nealsis" when I was a kid. Arok Wolvengrey notes, "It is only -sîs when -is is combined with something ending in …iy or …iw (for example, sîpiy becomes sîpîs or sîpîsis; piyêsiw- becomes piyêsîs, etc.). Many bird (and smaller creature) names end in -sîs, but this is derived from …isiw + -is > …isîs.

âsowaham 's/he crosses a river'.

âsowahonân 'a crossing [of the river]'. Would Gabriel's Crossing, near Batoche, be Gabriel otâsowahonân?

cîmân 'canoe', the way by which we travel on the rivers.

wêpâpotêw 'swept away by a current'.

ê-iskipêk sîpiy 'the river floods'.

nâsipêski 'riverbank' (maskêko-Cree): nâsipê 'go down to the water; go to fetch water'.

pimâšikamiw 'walk along the river' (maskêko-Cree).

kipwâpisko-sîpiy 'river dam'. Here, a root /kipw-/ referring to a 'blockage' or 'closure' is combined with the root -âpiskw- 'metal' (or, more traditionally, 'stone'). I think it means the metal that closes the river. Jean Okimâsis reminds us that kipwâpiskaha is 'lock it' (that is, 'stop/close with metal').

kâ-kipahamihk sîpiy ka-pôni-pimiciwahk 'river dam'; literally, 'the thing that closes the river to stop the flow of the river'.

kipahikanihk Fort Qu'Appelle, Saskatchewan; literally, 'at the enclosure' (often interpreted now as 'at the jail'). Grammatical note: -ihk makes the word locative, as with many place names. I think that the word originally meant 'at the weir'; the weir is what is enclosing the river, and today's Fort Qu'Appelle is the site of an historical Cree fishing weir.

pâwistik 'rapids'.

sâpociwan 'it flows through': sâpo- 'through'; -ciwan, a verb stem that denotes 'flowing' (you need to add a root morpheme, particle, or verb to the front of this verb stem to describe the flow of water).

âsokan 'bridge'; literally, 'the thing that allows one to cross'.

mâmihk 'downstream'. This could refer to any river. They use this term around Red Earth First Nation (kâ-mihkwaskîwahkâhk 'where the earth is red').

mâmihkiyiniwak 'Downstream People'. This referred to the nêhiyawak ('Crees') from the Battlefords area, around Fort Carlton and around Fort Pitt. The river referred to here is kisiskâciwani-sîpiy (Saskatchewan River).

natimihk 'upstream'.

natimîwiyiniwak 'Upstream People'. This referred to the people up the river, mainly in what is now Alberta.

pîhci-asiskîwi-ministikôšwa pipiskoc sîpîhk 'sandbar', a descriptive term (maskêko-Cree).

DAY 19

STAR WARS

I was one of the generation of wide-eyed awâsisak who saw *Star Wars* when it first came out in 1977. There were days when I would watch it five times in a row, and by the end of the day my stomach would be busting with popcorn. Even as a kid, when I heard Old Ben talk about the force with Luke Skywalker, I felt and sensed an affinity with those beliefs and some of the beliefs and stories that I heard growing up—although I too often imperfectly heard and understood these stories. I was so taken by *Star Wars* that I even went as Darth Vader for Hallowe'en in 1978. One of the things on my "bucket list" (and I don't mean KFC bucket list) is to translate *Star Wars Episode IV: A New Hope* into Cree. ahpô êtikwê ôtê nîkânihk.

mamâhtâwisiwin 'the Force'; this is actually an important reference to spiritual giftedness in Cree, and so, although some purists might object, it can also be applied to the way the Jedi use the Force.

mahti ka-wîcêwikowisin 'May the Force be with you'; mahti ka-wîcêwikowisinâwâw 'May the Force be with you all'; mahti ka-wîcêwikowisin, kâkikê 'May the Force be with you, always'.

tât pêtin 'Darth Vader'.

cêtay 'Jedi'. It is quite clear that the word cêtay is probably based on Cree okihcitâw 'worthy young men'.

kâ-kihci-cêtay-mâmawapicik 'Jedi Council'.

yêkawiyiniwak 'Sand People', 'Tusken Raiders'.

yêkaw-askiy 'Tatooine'.

. **iyinito-iyiniwak yêkaw-askîhk ohci** alternate description of 'Sand People' ('the Indigenous people of the Sand World').

kihci-mitâtahtomitanaw-kêhkêhk 'the *Millenium Falcon*'; literally, 'the Thousand Hawk'. That probably describes what's under the hood. Why would a spaceship have horse power? Hawk Power, I say!

nipiwin-acâhkos 'Death Star'.

wâskotê-sawêsk 'lightsaber'; literally, 'light sword'.

ayisiyinîhkânak 'Droids'; literally, 'artificial people'.

mosci-wâskotêkocinowin 'light speed'.

kihc-ôkimâskwêsis *Leia* 'Princess Leia'.

côwiy 'Chewie', 'Chewbacca'.

pôpahpit 'Boba Fett'.

kâ-môskîstâkêcik aniki kâ-nipahi-nâh-naspitâtocik *'Attack of the Clones'*; literally, 'when the Ones who resemble each other in an uncanny fashion attack'.

namôya êkonik ayisiyinîhkânak kâ-nâtawâpamacik 'These are not the droids you are looking for'—the famous words from Old Ben Kenobi.

omâtâhiwêw 'bounty hunter'; literally, 'tracker; one who tracks people'.

tâpwê mamâhtâwisiw awa 'The Force is strong with this one'.

ôpîwân kanôpiy 'Obi-Wan Kenobi'. His name does sound Cree, ma cî?

ôpîwân kanôpiy? kayâs aspin êwako wîhowin kâ-kî-pêhtamân, toni kayâs aspin. 'Obi-Wan Kenobi? That is a name that I have not heard in a long time, a long time'.

iskwayikohk wâpahki, mahti ka-wîcêwikowisinâwâw! 'Until tomorrow, may the Force be with you!'.

DAY 20

KENTUCKY FRIED CHICKEN

I have often thought that if Crees had saints, the Colonel would be one of them. Nothing says "I made it" more than when a young man can bring the extended family meal home to his family. In the old days, young men would go out on the land, hear the whispers of loons and unicorn buffalo, and at the end of the day would bring home wild game. But like many things, this has changed to some extent. Today, a young man will bring home "the bucket," and the Old Ones will sing "tâpwê, tâpwê miywâsin." I am sure that if the Colonel would have danced powwow, chicken dancing would have been his game.

kâ-kantakîwi-sâsisoht pâhkahâhkwân 'Kentucky Fried Chicken'. There is some variation in the stem 'to fry'. In Arok Wolvengrey's dictionary, *Cree Words*, one stem is listed as sâsâpiskisikê. I think this stem implies 'frying' by pan because of the root âpisk, which is embedded in it. Of course, KFC is fried using a deep fryer and a frying pan, so, in this case, a more basic form—sâsisa, 'fry it'—might be better. But since chicken is animate, we need to use sâsis(w)-. The -oht ending on sâsisoht implies that the verb is passive; that one who fries is unspecified and that the chicken must receive the action of the verb; for example, 'it is fried' in English. pâhkahâhkwân is the stem for 'chicken'.

micihcîsa kâ-nâh-nôkwâcikatêki 'finger-licking good' (my proposed term): micihcîsa 'fingers'; nôkwât 'to lick something'; nâh- intensifies the verb (in Cree grammar, this is called reduplication); once again that -ikatê ending means that the noun receives the action of the verb (that is, this is a passive verb structure, 'they [the fingers] are being licked'); -ki makes it plural and agrees with the plural 'fingers'. Actually, there is a more concise way to talk about this in Cree: sôpahcikê- 'to eat finger-licking good food'. The elegance of KFC.

pâhkahâhkwâniwiyâs mistikowat 'bucket of chicken': wiyâs 'meat'; mistikowat 'box, container made of wood', which might work as an extended metaphor.

pâhkahâhkwân mahkahk 'bucket of chicken': mahkahk 'tub' or 'barrel'.

pâhkahâhkwân mahkahkwêkin 'bucket of chicken'. This is another possible riff on this theme. In this case, the mahkahk 'barrel, tub' would be made out of -êkin, 'material, paper'.

kâya wîhtikowipayi! 'don't turn into a wîhtikow!' (that is, 'don't eat the last piece in the bucket!').

nîswâpisko-kîsikâw 'Toonie Tuesday'.

pâhkahâhkwân kîskwêwin 'craziness caused by chicken'.

kihci-pâhkahâhkwâni-nôtinikêwin 'the Great Chicken War'—the epic story of the great chicken wars between the Cree and their adversaries of yesteryear. A hide painting had the original KFC recipe on it. Through the years and wars, this painting exchanged hands many times.

pâhkahâhkwân-okimâw 'chicken boss', 'chicken chief' (the Colonel).

pâhkahâhkwân-okimâsis 'chicken prince', 'chicken sub-chief' (the branch manager or franchise boss).

awas, kâya kakwê-ocêmin! kitômitônân 'Don't try to kiss me! Your lips are greasy [from chicken]'.

sâsâsisikês 'deep-fryer guy', 'the guy in charge of the deep frying of chicken'. Many sâsâsisikêsak report that after about two years on the job, their vision begins to fade because of all of the grease.

wâh-wâhkôhtowi-mîcisowin 'extended family meal'.

DAY 21

FOOD

mîciwin is, of course, an important part of the lives of Cree people. My late father, Jermiah McLeod, and my Vandall grandfathers (although we always thought of them in the English term of uncles) were moose hunters and would often go on epic quests for food in the rolling woods of the parklands. I often think of the knowledge I don't have because I never acquired those skills.

One time, decades ago, my uncle, the late Burton Vandall, told me, there was a Thirst Dance on Whitefish Reserve. People always had a great deal of respect for the people on the Whitefish Reserve because of how hard they held on to everything Cree. During the ceremony, an Old Man got up and spoke of how young people were changing. He spoke of how they were not listening anymore, and how they had lost some of the old-time respect.

Another Old Man got up and said, "It is because of what they eat today."

This little story (âcimowinis) is a bit of insight into the ancestral knowledge that I hope someone else will explore in more detail. For now, this word list is a small attempt to document the importance of food in the lives of Cree people, and the Cree world.

mîciwin 'food'.

mîciso 'eat'. mîci means 'eat [something 'inanimate']' and mow is 'eat [something 'animate']'—remember that the idea of 'animate' does not necessarily mean something that has life. In Cree grammar, some things that are considered 'animate' (like pahkwêsikan 'bannock') are thought of as inanimate in English. The grammatical term 'animate' does not necessarily equate with "living"—perhaps we need a new way of communicating this concept.

piminawaso 'to cook; prepare a meal'.

kîsitêpo 'to cook feast food'.

kîsitêpowin 'feast food'.

piminawasowikamikos 'kitchen'. -(wi)kamik is a stem used to refer to any building or like structure. To describe the kind of building, you just add a verb in front of this stem. And, if you add -os to this construction, you have a small building or a room. (For more examples of this construction, *see* Day 22.)

kâh-kapatêstamâsowin 'buffet'. This is a noun (-win) built from a reflexive verb kapatêstamâso- 'ladle out food [for example, from a kettle] for oneself'. The reduplicated kâh- adds the idea of successive and repeated action (a number of different dishes). Thus, a 'buffet' or 'self-serve meal'. Bob Badger told me kašikêwikamikan would mean 'buffet' in Saulteaux (literally, 'greedy work' or 'greedy happening'). From the home office of Chris Hunter, 'buffet' was rendered as nanâtohko-mîcimowi-makosêwin ('feast of many different kinds of food'). I am getting hungry writing this.

sêkipacwâsi-mîciwin 'Chinese food'.

wâposo-mîciwin 'rabbit food' (Cree slang for salad).

oyâkan 'plate'.

asam 'feed him/her'.

mâtinawê-kîsikâw 'Saturday'; literally, 'the day of rations'. In some areas, this referred to Friday. It all depends on which day rations were issued.

DAY 22

BUILDINGS

Today our theme is buildings. I wanted to explore some possibilities of one root -(wi)kamik, which is added to words to describe various buildings. You just need to add verbs to the front of it to describe the building. Cree is like a giant Tetrus game, or puzzle, when you think about it, like a threading of all of the different parts into a whole. I have two quick notes here:

1. To talk about a room within a building. I have heard my family and others from the kistapinânihk (Prince Albert) area say -wikamikos, adding the -os diminutive ending to the 'building' to speak about a room in that building.

2. When people talk about a building as a location or destination, they add the locative to the noun; for example, cikâstêpayihcikêwikamikohk ê-kî-itôhtêyâhk, 'we went to the theatre'. The -ohk ending makes it locative; it indicates that we are talking about a location.

cikâstêpayihcikanikamik 'movie theatre'. The first part, cikâstê-, is interesting because it refers to 'shadow', and the rest of the initial stem, -payihcikan, is made up of –payi 'occur, happen, become, move' *plus* /-hc/ (or /-ht/), which suggests 'making (an inanimate thing)' and –ikan, indicating a thing produced from the action of the verb. So, a movie is a 'thing that is made of moving shadows', and the whole word, cikâstêpayihcikanikamik, means 'the building where shadows are made'. This Cree term, probably used a lot in the 1950s, sounds a lot like the term "flicker show," which was used in English at the same time.

mêtawêwikamik 'a house of games', 'a house/building of playing': mêtawê- 'to play'. The late Isaiah Bear from Muskoday First Nation used it to refer to 'pool halls'. It is also used to mean 'gymnasium', and some have suggested using it for theatres where 'plays' are performed.

atâwêwikamik 'store'; literally, 'the building where you buy things': atâwê- 'to buy'.

kihci-atâwêwikamik 'big store', used back in the long ago, kayâs ago days for forts (specifically the Hudson's Bay posts). Now we could push the metaphor to apply it to Walmart (that is our modern-day trading post, cah!).

kihci-atâwêwikamik ocacamiskâkês 'A Walmart greeter': atamiskaw- is the stem for 'to greet, to shake hands with someone', and adding -ikê to create atamiskâkê- makes the action general (that is, not mentioning a specific object). So when you say ocacamiskâkês, it means 'the little one [a term of affection] who shakes hands with people'.

minihkwêwikamik 'bar'; literally, 'drinking house': minihkwê- 'to drink'.

misatimowikamik 'horse barn'; literally, 'horse building'.

âhkosiwikamik 'hospital'; literally, 'sick house': âhkosi- 'to be sick'.

kîsinâtastêwikamik 'pawn shop'. I remember Kihci Bobby "The Bingo Caller" Kayseas and I once drove to Saskatoon to give a presentation. Being neechies, we picked up another neechie along the way, and during our journey on that warm spring day, the hitchhiker (owâstinikês) tried to sell us a dazzling ring. He even twirled it ever so gingerly. We got to town, and I would bet my last piece of bannock that neechie fella went to a kîsinâtastêwikamik and got some sôniyâw 'money'. I think there are two stems in the verb for 'pawn': kîsinât- 'unfortunate', and astê- 'to be placed'. The word for pawn shop, then, seems to mean 'the building where things are placed due to unfortunate circumstances'. But I also remember someone laughing when he described this word, saying it meant 'putting things down fast' on the counter, so maybe there's more to the riddle of this word.

Bobby Kayseas's father names a pawn shop in Saulteaux, mêskwatônakwakamik 'the trading place, the buying place'. I recognize the root mêskw-, which is found also in Cree, referring to 'exchange'. Arok Wolvengrey suggests, "Perhaps a Cree equivalent would be mêskotônikêwikamik 'exchange building.'"

sôskwânâtahikêwikamik 'hockey arena'. There are many variants of the word 'to skate'; one of them is sôskwanâtahikê-.

matotisân 'sweat lodge' (another kind of structure with different stems).

mîkiwâhp 'tipi' (another kind of structure with different stems).

sôniyâwikamik 'bank'; literally, 'money building': sôniyâw 'money'.

mosci-sôniyâwikamik 'money mart' (cah! I just made this up, but êtokwê, maybe mâskôc it might work).

âhtâtokamik 'casino'; literally, 'gambling place', as our Saulteaux brothers and sisters, the wind beneath our Cree wings, say it. How do we say casino in Cree? An equivalent for the Saulteaux form would be âstwâhtowikamik.

• • •

ê-nôhtê-âcimoyân ôma, anima âcimowinis, kâ-kî-ispayik ispîhk ê-kî-âtoskêyân Wanuskewin back in the kayâs ago days 'I want to tell a story, this little story, of when I worked at Wanuskewin back in the olden times'.

I and several of my Cree friends had been hired to work at Wanuskewin for the summer. We were all hired to work in the park for the summer and were all happy to have summer jobs. Every buck counted back in those days, and if wearing ribbon shirts and talking to tourists was a way we could get that buck, our little piece of the bannock pie, then by wîsahkêcâhk, we would.

One day, we knew German tourists were coming and were told to go out to the field and pitch a mîkiwâhp 'tipi'. As you probably know, our German friends have neechie-wut! 'a crazed admiration for neechies', and we didn't want to let them down. We ran out to that field, our field of dreams, and we thought that once we put up that tipi, they would come. That those tourists would come. We all ran out there, with tassles of ribbon fluttering in the wind and our smiles as big as Mac trucks.

We ran to the poles, but once we were there, we all took a deep breath. We had that feeling you have about a month after Christmas, when you realize you spent too much money and you try to pretend that everything will be okay. We all looked at each other, looking for a leader among us.

Finally, I asked them all if there was anyone who knew how to pitch a tipi. With the grim realization that we had been worn down by years of colonialism and living in Indian Affairs homes, we all looked to the ground, searching for answers that seemed to elude us. We felt like the people in *The Lord of the Rings* at Helm's Deep when the orcs are crashing at the walls. Just when we thought that all hope was lost, we felt the bewitching warmth of a light from the west, and we could hear the neigh of a horse. As that horse approached us, we opened our eyes.

wahwâ, we saw a great light that shone hope into the darkest places of our doubt, and then and only then we knew that we were okay. Joseph Naytowhow got off his steed and said, "tânisi, boysak. ka-kî-wîcihitakok cî?" ("Can I help you boys?"). Within minutes we had that tipi up, and for a few minutes, in that string of moments in time, we felt that we were all going to be okay. We knew that no Germans would be disappointed that day, and we knew that Karl May would have been proud of us all.

WEATHER

Whether we live in cities or towns, or on the reserve, the weather plays a key role in our lives. Weather words are often about the sky, but they also describe things around us, such as the snow, water, and forests. Cree weather terms do not simply mechanically describe the world around us; they describe the world through the lens of Cree-speaking people, and the philosophies embedded in our perceptions of the world and the way in which we tell stories.

tânisi ê-isi-wêpahk? 'what is the weather like?'; literally, 'how is it being flung?'.

kâ-kitocik 'they are calling'. This refers to the Thunderbirds (piyêsiwak) and is used to describe the sound of thunder. I always had an interest in words related to thunder because my ancestor, the original McLeod, was named nîkân-isi, which means 'the foremost Being', a metaphorical way of talking about Thunderbirds. He had another name, mahkiyoc 'the one with the big body' (understood as 'the tall one'). He was the father of Abel McLeod, who was heavily involved in the League of Indians.

I remember I learned the phrase kâ-kitocik from the late Edward Caisse (from Green Lake). He was Cree Métis and taught me a great deal. Much of the Cree language has been maintained by the Métis. This makes sense because so many Métis have strong connections with land and territory, and (generally speaking) they did not go to residential schools as the Cree did.

miskwamiy pahkisin 'hail': miskwamiy 'ice'; pahkisin 'it [animate] falls down'. Ice is animate in Cree.

kîstin 'tornado'. An Innu band from the 1990s was called Kashtin, which is their way of saying 'tornado'. Other words for tornado in Plains Cree include pistôsiw, and variations on that.

kimiwan 'it is raining'.

pahkipêscâsin 'it is drizzling'.

sîkipêstâw 'it is pouring' (that is, heavy rain).

ispanaskwan 'high clouds'. This would include the root isp-, which is also present in ispimihk 'up; above'.

takwanaskwan 'rolling-in clouds'. This would include the root takw-, which is also present in takosin 's/he arrives'.

payipâstêw 'the sun shines through a hole in the clouds'.

ê-miyo-kîsikâk 'it is a beautiful day'; in Anishinaabemowin this would be communicated with minogiizhigat (mino-kîšikat in Saulteaux).

kisâstêw 'it is hot' (that is, temperature from sunshine). This is gzhaate in Anishnaabemowin, and the Saulteaux form is kišâhtê. The use of "k" and "g" in spelling Cree and Ojibwe dialects should not be equated directly to English /k/ and /g/ sounds. The symbols represent sounds specific to each of these languages.

kihci-kisâstêw 'incredibly hot'.

kisinâw 'it is very cold'. In Anishinaabemowin, that would be gzinaa and in Saulteaux, kišinâ.

DAY 24

DIRECTIONS

Most neechies can find their way around, but I am directionally challenged. My far-paddling, canoe-riding, and horse-fighting ancestors must laugh at me. "wahwâ, ê-itwêcik, wâpam kôsisiminaw, mêtoni kitimâkisiw. kâh-kapê wanisin!" "'Look at our grandson, he is truly pitiful. He is always lost!'" With that being said, here are some words for directions.

ispimihk 'above'. This can also be used today for 'upstairs'. In the Anglican Bible, this was used to translate the idea of the heavens.

nîhc-âyihk 'below'; also used for 'downstairs'.

capasîs 'below' (another word for 'below' or 'lower', etc.).

tahkohc 'on top'.

sîpâhk 'under, beneath'.

namahcîhk '[on the] left'. It always took me a long time to remember this word for some reason. A left-handed person is namahcîs. I am still trying to figure out what this stem really means, but it sounds like the negative nama is a part of this.

kihciniskêhk '[on the] right'. Once again, I am still trying to figure out what this stem means, but it appears to include the elements kihci- 'great' and -nisk- 'hand; lower arm'. Was there a similar bias toward right handers?

kîwêtinohk 'north'. Interestingly, the word for north has the stem kîwê 'to go home'. While I have spent a lot of time working on the language and stories of the North, I am not a bushman. I remember one time, R.J. Morin from Île-à-la-Crosse told me that you could tell which way was north by the way the tree grew: the strongest winds were from the north. So many people like R.J. have such a deep and profound sense of the land, in a way that I don't but that I respect greatly.

sâwanohk 'south'.

pahkisimôtâhk 'west'; 'in the direction where the sun sets'.

sâkâstênohk 'east'; 'the direction in which the sun [or really, 'the light'] appears'; ê-pê-sâkâstêk, meaning 'coming light', is one way to refer to 'the dawn'.

wâpanohk 'east'; 'the direction of the dawn'.

itâskonikê 'to point the pipe' (in different directions). One time, my câpân, Peter Vandall (kôkôcîs), was with his grandfather, wîhtikôhkân, on Sandy Lake Reserve. wîhtikôhkân had a house made of wood slabs, and there were some openings. There was a very strong wind. wîhtikôhkân ê-kî-itâskonikêt 'pointed his pipestem and prayed'. The wind stopped, and they were okay. There is more to the story, but I just wanted to share a little bit of it now.

kwayask nîkân isi 'straight ahead'.

nâway ôtê 'behind'.

nîkân ôtê 'the future'; literally, 'over here in the front'.

DAY 25

IMITATIONS OR FAKES

Today I want to explore the ending –hkân, which occurs at the end of many nouns. This element makes the verb or noun in front of it 'an imitation' (or in some cases, you could translate that as 'fake'). It is a good Cree Jedi word trick to know because it is a useful tool in compounding âniskoscikêwin. In the heart of the Cree language is this process of compounding. Also key to Cree is the way metaphor functions: -hkân extends the meaning of the word it appends to other possibilities and threads together other possibilities of sound. The vowels before this ending are often long, depending on the shape of the word that it is joined to.

sîpîhkân 'canal'. From sîpiy 'river'; literally, 'fake river', 'imitation river'.

okimâhkân from okimâw 'chief'; literally, 'a fake, imitation, or appointed chief'. The word is an embodiment of the Cree experience of colonialism. It holds the idea that the chief's authority is imposed on the people from the outside by another government and system. A chief that has been appointed rather than chosen and trained in the traditional way.

miskîsikohkâna 'glasses'; literally, 'artificial eyes'.

nîcimosihkân 'a fake girlfriend' (an Internet girlfriend that you only talk to but never really meet, cah!).

pîsimohkân 'a clock', 'a watch'; 'an imitation sun', from pîsim 'sun'.

askîhkan 'reserve land'; 'an imitation earth', from askiy 'earth'. pîhtikwahânapiwiyin (Poundmaker) at Treaty Six at pêhonânihk (Fort Carleton) wondered how the government could divide up the lands into small portions. I think he was anticipating this word and this concept when he spoke. askîhkân is sometimes used as well for farmland or even a measurement of land like 'acre'.

manitôhkân from manitow 'spirit being'; 'imitation spirit'. There were small carvings/statues that were found in forests and on the sides of hills. People would put cistêmâw 'tobacco', sênipânak 'ribbons', and necklaces on these. Family oral history speaks of the manitôhkânak as kâ-kanawêyihtahkik askiy 'the ones who take care of the land'.

wîhtikôhkân 'imitation wîhtikow'. This was the name of one of my grandfathers. He was the brother to kinosêw and mostos. The name is a profound one and refers to the society of the Crees (and Saulteaux) called wîhtikôhkânak (wîntikôhkânak). These are contraries who do things backward. Many anthropologists got this wrong completely and thought they were wîhtikowak, or 'clowns'. It goes to show you that all of the parts of a Cree word are important in determining nisitohtamowin 'understanding'.

ayisinîhkân 'imitation person'; 'droid', 'robot'. (*See* Day 19.)

tâpasinahikêpayihcikan 'copying machine' (Xerox for old-timers like me). The stems here are: tâpasinahikê 'to draw', to copy'; -payi 'suddenly, automatically'; -ht (or -hc), which marks causation by adding an agent and making the previous verb an active process; and –ikan, which refers to an object or thing described by all of the other elements that occur before it. In this case, the ending is -ikan, not –hkân, and this is a very important difference that is often missed in non-standard or English-based spellings. The machine, the thing (-ikan), is making copies, but the machine is not itself a copy of something else.

DAY 26

FUNNY CREE EXPRESSIONS (PART 1)

I think that it would be hard to talk Cree and learn Cree and to never laugh. Laughing seems to be a national pastime of the Crees. Indeed, there could probably be a whole book about funny Cree expressions. While we were telling jokes and drinking tea, the British marched westward with stern faces, in neat and ordered lines. Well, I think I would rather have great jokes than an empire, but maybe ... cah!

Here we go! Hoka hey!

mahkatay pôskwatê-kitohcikan 'guitar'. I heard my uncle, the late Burton Vandall, say this once. It means 'the big belly with a hole in the middle that makes music'. Cree is a natural language of tomfoolery.

pwâkamo-pahkwêsikan 'pizza'. Another one I heard my old uncle say. It means 'the throw-up bread'. Sorry to kill your love of pizza, but that is what some of the old nêhiyawak thought of it. Visually, I guess, it just made sense of it.

kinoyaw-otâpânâsk 'bus'; literally, 'the long body vehicle'. Another one from my late Uncle Burton. I would like to thank my old uncle for helping me with Cree.

môniyâw-matotisân 'sauna'; literally, 'a white-man sweat'. My family uses this expression when they want to sauna.

pîwâpisk-piyêsîs 'plane'; literally, 'metal bird'. Believe it or not, I found this in a word list somewhere long ago. It makes sense, and it makes sense that old Crees would simply extend the old metaphors.

mistikowat kâ-pîkiskwêmakahk 'radio'; literally, 'the box that talks'.

osâm-âcimowin 'poetry'; literally, 'the story that overdoes it'.

iskotê-pimiy 'fire lard'. That is a word I know for gas. Maybe if the price of gas keeps going up, we could make sêhkêpayîsak 'cars' powered by lard.

oskâtâsk 'carrot'. The Oji-Cree interpret this word as 'new legs': oski- 'new'; oskâta 'his/her legs'. They see carrots as new legs. Of course, there is the oskâtâsko-sîpiy (Carrot River), which runs just south of where I grew up.

awiyak kâ-ohpikihat 'the one you are raising'; if the person you are with is much younger then you, some Cree wise-guyz or wise-ladieszes might say this to you.

ê-sâh-sâpopêpicikêt 'dabbing bingo'. One time, at the legendary Carnival Bingo in kistapinânihk (Prince Albert), someone said this to another Old Man. The one Old Man said, cah! (meaning, *What you talkin' 'bout, Willis?*). It literally means 'making something wet through and through'. Cree is always walking the edge of the risqué. That is probably why, as Tomson Highway said, we are the sexiest people in the world.

ê-sôskwâ-wêpinipicikêhk 'curling': sôskwâ 'smooth, slippery'; wêpin- 'to throw, hurl'; -picikê, denoting a vigorous action described by the preceding stems. I have always understood it to mean 'an active process'. This was a word of my câpân, Peter Vandall, from yêkawiskâwikamâhk (Sandy Lake). A variation on this term, coined for the Olympic commentary included -âpisk 'stone': ê-sôskwâ-wêpinâpiskinikêhk literally refers to 'slide-throwing rock by hand'.

DAY 27

SPRING

The spring was an important time for Cree people. When the ice on the rivers began to melt, the people knew that the rivers would be ready for travel again, and that they could travel long distances on them. In the spring, in my territory and among my relatives from around Sandy Lake, people would get syrup from birch trees, make canoes, and have a dog feast. The dogs were so important to the Cree people that they honoured them in this ceremony. Also, it must be remembered that the women owned the dogs.

Spring was a time of opening, a time when the water opened, and when the land opened up to reveal its gifts of medicine and plants.

sîkwan 'spring'. I understand this word to mean the time of spring after the main thaw. In Anishinaabemowin, it is ziigwan.

miyoskamin 'spring'. But this term means the initial spring thaw, when the water is flowing and the snow is slowly melting.

sâkipakâw 'the leaves are budding'.

sâkipakâwi-pîsim 'the month where the leaves are budding' (usually used for May).

kîhtwâm piyêsîsak nikamowak 'the birds are singing again': kîhtwâm 'again'; piyêsîsak 'birds'; nikamo 'to sing'.

sîpiy sôhkêciwan 'the river flows strongly': sîpiy 'river'; sôhkê- 'strong, hard'; -ciwan 'to flow'.

nîpinaskamikâw 'bare ground after melting snow'.

kôniwâpoy 'water from melting snow'.

wâposo-kîsikâw 'Easter'; literally, 'rabbit day'.

kipikwâciwamahcihon cî? 'do you feel frisky?'.

sîkwani-nahascikêwin 'spring cleaning'.

DAY 28

HOW SWEETGRASS BECAME CHIEF (PART I)
FROM *PLAINS CREE TEXTS*

Here is another set of terms from the out-of-print classic book *Plains Cree Texts*. One interesting point is that the narratives in this volume are focused more on history, politics, and military events, whereas the other more widely available book, *Sacred Stories of the Sweetgrass Cree*, is focused on the âtayôhkêwina, the 'sacred stories' of wîsahkêcâhk. The following terms come from an interesting story about when wîhkasko-kisêyin became a chief.

otinêw misatimwa 'he took a horse': otin- 'to take [someone or something animate]'; mistatimwa 'horse' in the obviative form (it is the object of the verb and less topical than the one who is taking the horse [that is, Sweetgrass himself]). A general note in regards to classical Cree storytelling: often the storyteller speaks in the present tense.

kitâpahkan 'spyglass': kitâpahkê- 'to watch, to look, to observe'. Here, the -kê verbal ending alternates with a -kan ending for the noun. This is a slightly older pattern, which is the same as the -ikê/-ikan alternation we've seen before. The word as a whole, then, literally means 'the thing that allows someone to see, watch, observe'.

ayisiyiniwa ê-nanâtawâpamâyit 'he was looking for people': ayisiyiniw 'person; people'. In this case, both the one looking and the people are in the obviative.

kiskêyimêw ayâhciyiniwa 'he knew him for a Blackfoot': kiskêyim 'to know someone' (transitive animate verb stem); ayâhciyiniw 'Blackfoot' (literally, 'someone who is different', 'a stranger'). Note: in the Anglican Bible the term ayâhciyiniwa was used for 'Gentile'. It would be interesting to know how Gentile was translated into Blackfoot (and indeed other Indigenous languages).

pîhtasô 'to load a gun'.

môskîstaw 'to attack someone'.

matwêwêw 'it [for example, a gun] sounds off'.

pâskisikan 'gun'.

nêhiyaw ê-têhtapit 'the Cree on his horse'. têhtapi- literally means 'to sit on top', but it is used to refer to 'riding' or 'mounting' a horse.

itisahw- 'to drive someone toward someplace, somewhere' (with, in this setting, military-tactical connotations). This verb is also related to "to send" (itisaha 'send it').

DAY 29

FUNNY CREE EXPRESSIONS (PART 2)

After collecting the jokes that came in from those who read and enjoyed the Day 26 entries, I decided to put together another list of humorous Cree sayings. I think these point not only to the humour of Cree people but also to the dynamic nature of the Cree language, which allows us to describe contemporary experiences and events.

kîskwêpasokan 'marijuana'; literally, 'the crazy smoke'. Darren Okemaysim told me this one in the kayâs ago days of the Saskatchewan Indian Federated College. Note: -kan is not as commonly added to an unmodified VAI stem as say, -win, which would be a more normal ending here. However, -win would indicate a process more than a thing.

kîskwêpasoskîs 'stoner'.

wâsakâmâpoy 'wine'. I heard this once upon a time from Neil Sapp, I think. It is literally 'the pass-around liquid'.

ê-âh-hoka-hey-payihot 'Powwowing it up'.

nôkwahcikan 'hickey'.

nâh-nôkwahcikês 'one who administers hickeys often'.

nôcinâpêwê 'hunt men' (to go snagging men).

nôcihiskwêwê 'hunt women' (to go snagging women).

nôcinâpêwê-akohp 'a snagging blanket' (when men are being snagged).

nôcihiskwêwê-akohp 'a snagging blanket' (when women are being snagged).

pinko otêpwêw 'bingo caller'.

nimosôm owîhowin 'my mosôm's name', referring to how Treaty documents were signed by some Cree people; also, the "X" pattern in bingo.

acâhko-otâpânâsk 'sputnik' (pattern in bingo); literally, 'the star vehicle'.

sâpopêpicikan 'bingo dabber'; literally, 'the thing that makes something wet'.

cimasowask 'Viagra'; literally, 'erection medicine'.

mošê-tî 'straight tea' ('naked tea'). Arok "Magic Man" Wolvengrey notes, "Because of the soundalike Cree word stem –tiy 'buttocks', this is definitely going to elicit the requisite chuckles, and then some…".

pišâkanâpî-omicâs 'thong'; literally, 'stringy underwear'.

pwêkito-pâhpiwin 'a laugh that causes you to fart'.

pwêkito-mîciwin 'Mexican food'; literally, 'fart food'.

pwêkicôs 'the one who farts a lot'.

pwêkito-maskihkiy 'the farting medicine' (the medicine that caused kistêsinaw—Elder Brother—to fart to the moon).

okimâw-otâpânâsk 'limousine'; literally, 'the king car'.

kihci-pâh-pimp-ihowin 'big pimpin'. Note: this term still probably needs work. I just constructed it around the same verb-ending structure that I have heard people use when they talk about 'being a rockstar'.

kîsikâw-sôniyâwasinahikan 'per diem cheque'.

DAY 30

HOW SWEETGRASS BECAME CHIEF (PART 2)
FROM *PLAINS CREE TEXTS*

This is a continuation of the cluster of words examined on Day 28. Working with original texts/narratives—in this case, stories told by kâ-kîsikâw-pîhtokêw—is key, because it helps to give the context from which the words emerged. I think that Cree language studies will only increase in power as we move more toward looking at the stem meanings of words and also put words in a narrative context.

nawaswât- 'to pursue [someone]'. The imperative form would be nawaswâs 'chase him/her'.

sîpîsis 'creek'; literally, 'little river'.

pahkopê- 'to enter the water, to wade'.

wîhkwêskaw- 'to surround someone' (with military-tactical connotations).

wâtihkân 'trench' (as in warfare). wâtihkê- means 'to dig a hole', and the word also can have non-military connotations, as in mahihkan-wâtihkân 'wolf-den'. Another word, mônahikê-, means 'to dig a hole' (toward some purpose or end). It is used in the context of mining but also refers to the digging action of a weasel (in the James Smith dialect). kâ-mônahikos (literally, 'The Digger') was the name of a legendary Cree chief from Alberta. One man, iskotêw, was there when kâ-mônahikos used his powers of making holes to escape the Blackfoot near maskihkiy-astotin (Medicine Hat). I heard this story many times from the late Charlie Burns.

simâkanis-okimâw Bloomfield translates this as 'officer', but it would be perhaps better translated as 'one who has authority over soldiers'. Perhaps a general could be kihci-simâkanis-okimâw. simâkanis now refers to police officers, presumably because they serve analogous functions. simâkanisihkân refers to a veteran (and connotes 'he who is like a soldier'). I think that the -hkân ending does not always have to be translated as 'fake' or 'artificial', but perhaps as something analogous to the noun in question.

nîkânohtê- 'to go in the lead': nîkân 'in front'; -ohtê is the stem for 'to walk'. In the same way, pimohtê- 'to walk' really means 'to walk along', with the root pim- indicating a straight or progressive fashion in which the walking is accomplished.

tahkam- 'to stab [someone]' (in the context of the story, it is 'stabbing with a knife').

nipah- 'to kill [someone]'.

manisamaw- 'to take [someone's] scalp in combat', though it is literally 'cut it from or for [someone]'. There is an interesting story of atimwâyow (atimoyoo or Dog Tail), which I heard years ago. They say that atimoyoo would ê-kwêskîmot 'change form' to a coyote (I think), and during combat would kill dogs of the enemy. During the Thirst Dance, in the older times, people would present scalps taken. atimoyoo would present the tails of dogs (rivals that he had slain).

DAY 31

TIM HORTONS

Many neechies get their neechie fuel from Tim Hortons. In fact, many Cree children think that Tim Horton is their uncle who is married to their Auntie Sally Ann. Cree, like all living languages, describes the world around us and our experiences within that world, including the restaurants and coffee places we go to. In the following list are words that can be used to help describe Tim Hortons.

cim-ôtan 'Tim Hortons'.

miyin nicimîmisa! 'give me my Timmies!'. A variant could be nicimîsima.

pihkahtêwâpoy 'coffee'.

pihkahtêwâpôhkân 'decaffeinated coffee'; literally 'fake coffee'. Or you could say, tâpiskôc pihkahtêwâpoy 'it's like coffee'.

manahikan 'cream'.

sîwinikan 'sugar'; sôkâw also means 'sugar'.

nîswâw, nîswâw 'double, double'.

iyinitowâpoy 'regular'.

pêyak manahikan 'one cream'.

sôskwâwâpoy 'smoothie'; or maybe just sôskwâpoy.

sâpokocinowin 'drive-throı

DAY 32

STORIES

Fortunately, we live in a time when a great many people are making strong efforts to learn their Indigenous languages. Cree is one language that is certainly still within our reach, and we are pleased to have many storytellers around us who are waiting for us to visit. They have a great deal of information to share with us. I thought it would be useful, as we engage in our journey to learn Cree and to get better at speaking it, to list various words about stories.

âcimowina 'stories'; everyday stories, accounts of events.

kihci-âcimowina 'the great stories'; the stories of warfare between the Crees and Blackfoot.

âcimisowina 'stories about oneself'; could be thought of as autobiographies.

wawiyatâcimowina 'humourous tales'.

kakêskihkêmowina 'counselling stories'; one place where these stories are told is at round dances.

kiskisiyâpiya 'threads of memory'.

manâcimowinê- 'to collect stories'. kayâs mâna nêhiyawak ê-kî-manâcimowinêcik *Saskatchewan Indian Cultural Centre*ihk. 'A long time ago, the Crees gathered stories at the Saskatchewan Indian Cultural Centre'. I used to travel with my mosôm John R. McLeod in his Olds. He drove all over recording people with a reel-to-reel recorder.

mêstâtayôhkanêsin 's/he runs out of sacred stories'. I want to use this term in a novel I am writing, called *Dreaming Blue Horses*, about post-1885 realities.

kwêskî-âcimowina I just made this one up, but maybe it could refer to 'stories where people change their lives around'. Another possibility would be kwêskâtisiwâcimowina.

kiskisom- a VTA verb meaning 'to remind [someone]', which is what stories do.

DAY 33

THE GOOSE

One thing that adds to the beauty of the Cree language, I think, is the richness in terms of dialectical variation. One young man who has inspired a large number of people to speak Cree is Chris Hunter. Chris speaks the maskêko dialect of Cree. Not only do I think it is important to gather various dialectal variations of words, but I also think it is important to document some of the cultural forces that animate these words.

We have old Cree roots in the knowledge and words of the maskêko-Cree. For example, just as the horse plays a role in animating the world of Plains Cree, the goose animates maskêko-Cree. Here is a small glimpse into this ancestral wisdom couched in goose terminology.

ašowêhikan 'ambush place'; 'cover or blind for hunting'.

niskihkân 'decoy'; literally, 'fake goose'.

niska-nîmiwin 'Goose Dance'.

niska 'goose'. Name of main female character from Joseph Boyden's novel, *Three Day Road*.

niska-mîkwan 'goose feather'; niska-mîkwanis 'little goose feather'.

kihci-niska 'great goose'; 'boss goose'; 'Canada goose'.

nôsê-niska 'female goose'.

nâpê-niska 'male goose'.

niskišiš; niskisis 'gosling'.

niska-cahkîstêhikan 'goose beak'; literally, 'goose stabber, poker'.

niski-wâwa 'goose eggs'.

apisci-niska 'lesser Canada goose'; or a different, smaller species of goose.

niska-misit 'goose foot'; or simply, niskisit.

pêci-kîwê-pimihamowak 'they come flying home'; spring migration. pî-kîwêwak nihkak is Saulteaux for 'the geese coming home'.

kihci-piponi-pimihamowak 'they take their great winter flight'; fall migration.

nihka 'goose', in Saulteaux.

DAY 34

BIRDS

The storyscape of Cree-speaking people is full of birds. We think of such important birds as the piyêsiw 'Thunderbird' and, of course, the eagle. The vocabulary describes birds not only in terms of species but also in terms of their movements. I think that it would be very worthwhile to document more of these words in the style of Elders' workshops that my late mosôm John R. McLeod used to help facilitate in the 1970s. The list of words below is rather long because of the extensive input from people to my Facebook page. kinanâskomitinâwâw 'I'm grateful to all of you'.

piyêsîs 'bird'.

(â)môsi-piyêsîs 'hummingbird'; this is a word used on James Smith Cree Nation that is a variation on the more common word for hummingbird, âmowi-piyêsîs; literally, 'bee bird'.

kihiw 'eagle'; usually identified as the golden eagle.

mikisiw 'eagle'; possibly preferred in northern Cree, but in part this may be due to its common association with the bald eagle. migiizi is 'eagle' in Anishinaabemowin.

kêhkêhk 'hawk'.

sâkwahtamow 'red-tailed hawk'.

mîkwan 'feather'.

pihêw 'prairie chicken'. pihêwisimowin 'chicken dance' is an old dance of the okihcitâwak.

wacistwan 'nest'.

mitahtahkwan 'wing'.

taswêkakocin 'it glides through the air with wings spread'.

pihpihcêw 'robin'.

sîsîp 'duck'.

pasakwâpisimowin 'the Shut-Eye Dance', in which wîsahkêcâhk tricks the ducks and geese.

kâhkâkiw 'raven'. There are many stories about the intelligence of ravens.

âhâsiw 'crow'. The same goes for crows.

pâskâwiho 'hatch'; a verb that describes 'bursting through the eggshell'.

pâskâwihowi-pîsim 'June' or 'the Egg-Hatching Moon'.

mîcaskosîs 'swallow'.

pâhkahâhkwân 'chicken'.

pâhpâstêw 'large woodpecker'.

pâhpâscêsis 'small woodpecker'.

ocicâhk 'crane'.

misihêw 'turkey'; literally, 'big prairie chicken'.

pîscêwaciwasôs 'meadowlark'; literally, 'the little one who boils it until it foams'. The name does not describe what the bird does, but the word can be sung to the song of the meadowlark. mâmaskâc! Music to my ears.

DAY 35

EDUCATION

Education is of strong importance to Cree people in terms of our history and culture. In the early days of the League of Indians, there were great efforts put in place to stop residential schools. Indeed, it was one of its key focuses (along with Treaties). I think that these old leaders knew that resolving the issues arising from residential schools were at the core of Indigenous peoples regaining our sovereignty and collective well-being. I think of how these leaders would ride horses, sometimes for hundreds of kilometres, to attend political meetings, at a time when Canadian society was very repressive toward Indigenous people. Yet, because of the efforts of these leaders, and also the efforts of our grandmothers who kept us clothed and nourished us with language and healed us with medicines, we survived and are now able, in this time, to continue the retrieval of our culture and language.

iyinito-iyiniw-kiskêyihtamowin 'Indigenous Knowledge'. This might be one way to coin this common expression in academia. kiskêyihtamowin is 'knowledge'; I know that iyinito-iyiniwak is one way of expressing 'Indigenous people'. The iyinito- stem represents

the 'ordinary, regular, or prototypical best example [of something]';
thus, 'feast grease' is called iyinito-pimiy, and iyinito-kinosêw is
the 'most common fish' (which varies by region, but for many is
'pike' or 'jackfish').

kiskinwahamâsowin 'education'. This is a noun formed by adding
-win (indicating a general process) to the verb stem kiskinwahamâso-.
This is, in turn, built with several meaningful elements: kiskinw- 'to
guide' *plus* -ah 'instrumental' form the word kiskinwah- 'to teach
something'; -amaw is a benefactive indicating the ones being
taught; -iso is the reflexive, meaning the action is done for one's own
benefit. This word implies that people have to find things out for
themselves. It represents a very different philosophy of education
than sometimes exists.

kiskinwahamâtowin 'education'. An alternate form, substituting
the reciprocal -ito for the reflexive -iso. In this case, education is
a mutual process in which we learn from one another, rather than
simply a one-way path from teacher to learner. Again, this is a very
different philosophy of education than the Western model.

ê-iskôliwit 's/he goes to school'. A term that was used in north-
eastern Saskatchewan (for example, James Smith Reserve) and
farther east as well.

okiskinwahamâkêw 'teacher'.

môniyâwi-kiskêyihtamowin 'European learning'.

kihci-kiskinwahamâtowikamik 'university'. The stems break
down like this: kihci- 'great' and sometimes with the implication

of 'highest' (of whatever is being described); kiskinwahamaw 'to educate someone', really 'to guide', 'to point out'; -ito is a reciprocal process including all parties involved; -wikamik 'a building'. I would question this term, though—why would the university be the "highest" point of knowing? Why wouldn't tradition and classical places of learning have equal weight? Maybe that is why some refer to 'university' as misi-kiskinwahamâtowikamik, using misi- 'big' rather than kihci- 'great'.

masinahikan 'book': masinahikê 'to write; to make a mark'; masinipayihcikê 'to take pictures of film' or 'to publish'.

ê-kî-koskonikawiyahk 'we were woken up'. This term was used sometimes in the 1970s when people were gathering stories at the Saskatchewan Indian Cultural Centre.

kêhtê-aya ê-ohpikihikot 'one raised by Old People'.

nama kîkway ê-kiskêyihtamân 'I know nothing': nama kîkway 'nothing'; kiskêyiht- 'to know'. A classic Cree expression: kêhtê-ayak are wise enough to understand, while the rest of us still think we're so smart.

kiskinohamâkosi 'to learn, to be a student'.

DAY 36

HOW SWEETGRASS BECAME CHIEF (PART 3)
FROM *PLAINS CREE TEXTS*

Today, we again look at terms from another version of "How Sweetgrass Became Chief" as it was recorded in *Plains Cree Texts*. Previous examinations took place on Days 28 and 30. The phrases listed here are from the story told by Simon Mimikwas. mimikwâs is recorded as another word for 'butterfly' (along with kamâmak) and is the word used for the same in Saulteaux.

One historical note: wîhkasko-kisêyin was the principal chief of the River People of the Crees and Saulteaux in the North Battleford area. He was an historically important leader and helped to anchor the people in their land and place. He was also a good friend of mistahi-maskwa.

wîhkasko-kisêyin 'Old Man Sweetgrass': wîhk- 'sweet'; -askw- is the root for 'plant, herb, medicine'; kisêyin is a shortened form of kisêyiniw 'Old Man', which can be broken down into kisê- 'kind' and iyiniw 'person, being'. Note: inini means 'man' in Anishinaabemowin. There was a younger Sweetgrass, his son, and thus that is why he was referred to as 'Old Man Sweetgrass'.

sakimês 'mosquito'; the source of Sweetgrass's power, his pawâkan.

kitimâkisi 'to be pitiful'. The mosquito tells wîhkasko-kisêyin that he (Sweetgrass) is pitiful, and that he (the mosquito) will help him. (Note how the English 'he' could easily be misinterpreted in the previous sentence? In Cree grammar, the obviative is a category that disambiguates two different third-person referents and thus avoids that problem.)

pêkopayi 'to wake up [suddenly]'; koskon means to 'wake [someone] up'; waniskâ means 'to rise, to get up'; and wâpâsi is a verb stem that means 'to be an early riser'.

sakimêsa ohpihâyiwa ohtawakâhk ohci 'A mosquito flew from his ear': -htawakay- 'ear' occurs with –ihk, marking it as a location; ohci means 'from' (a key word for constructing Cree sentences). Note that 'mosquito' and the verb 'to fly' are in the obviative form and distinguish the mosquito from the one whose ear is being referred to. The prefix o- indicates the third-person possessive, but not in the obviative, so the possessor is the main topic, as distinct from the mosquito.

mîkiwâhp 'tipi' (traditional Plains Cree and Saulteaux lodge). Women owned them, and people would paint them in a sacred manner.

natimihk 'in the west'. Bloomfield translates it this way, but really, the word means 'upstream', referring to the kisiskâciwani-sîpiy (Saskatchewan River). Prominent landforms were commonly used to reference the directions.

môswasiniy 'bullet'; literally, a 'moose stone', a metaphor or 'thought weaving' for moose hunting. A linguistic remembrance of being a woodlands people.

môhkota 'to shape bullets' (referring to musket ordnance). Traditionally, this term would mean 'whittle it, plane it' and was perhaps originally used relative to the making of arrows, and thus transferred to the production of bullets.

sipwêpayi 'to ride away'; in this story, the term refers to horses, but today it could mean 'to drive away in a car or other vehicle'.

DAY 37

CREE NARRATIVE MEMORY

Now that my father has passed, and also Charlie Burns, I value more than ever the stories and the pieces of language that they taught me. The stories that my late father told me organically emerged in the spaces of days. The stories rested and grew in the spaces between the sober sound of a midnight bingo caller and the belly-cracking laughter of a Cree telling his or her last joke on earth. These stories spoke of various places, of various people, and of various events. To use Louise Halfe's metaphor, these stories were like blue marrow of the body of the collective memory of nêhiyawak. These stories are like water that constantly cleans the stones of our memory if we tend to them often. To the people who told me these stories, I will forever be grateful, and I will do my best to document these stories, so a narrative legacy will be left for those who come after us. It is for this reason that I wrote *Cree Narrative Memory*, and for this reason, I would like to share with you some of the words (and small glimpses of the stories behind the words) that I collected on my journey.

nikisêyiniwikwêmês 'Old Man Buffalo': ni- 'my'; kisêyiniw 'Old Man' (literally, 'kind being'); -kwêmês 'namesake'. This is the Grandfather Buffalo at the centre of the classical Cree/Saulteaux story of mistasiniy. His name stresses the kinship between the buffalo and the boy, and also between the Crees and the buffalo.

pâstâhowin 'trangression'; 'bad karma'. Perhaps if someone does not share their food, then one could say, ê-pâstâhot. To put it into common English, "What goes around, comes around."

mistanaskowêw 'Badger Call' (or 'Calling Badger' or 'Badger Voice'). The Cree who was gifted in syllabics by the Creator.

ê-kî-mâyahkamikahk 'when it went wrong'. The Cree and Cree-Métis word to describe the tragic events of 1885.

kâ-miyikowisiyahk 'what the powers have given us'. Some of the Crees of old said this when they negotiated Treaty. They said, "There is no way that the Queen can replace kâ-miyikowisiyahk."

kawâhkatos 'lean/skinny/hungry one'. An important Cree leader who questioned the "buying of land" at Treaty Four negotiations. I have a long story about this, which my late mosôm John R. McLeod collected in the 1970s.

kotâwîwak 'they enter the ground', referring to the retreating of Beings from the surface of the earth after everything changed for the Crees, Saulteaux, and Métis.

mêmêkwêsiwak 'the Little People'. (For more, *see* Day 15.)

oskâpêwis 'Elder's helper', or apprentice, like a Jedi padawan; literally, 'a young man'. As best as I can figure, okihcitâwiskwêw could be the female equivalent of this.

ê-kî-mistâpâwêhisocik 'They drown themselves'; said of the buffalo when the world was changing. My câpân kôkôcîs had stories of this.

DAY 38

HOW SWEETGRASS BECAME CHIEF (PART 4)
FROM *PLAINS CREE TEXTS*

Following are more terms from the story, as told by Simon Mimikwas (*see* Day 36). This story discusses the way in which Sweetgrass rises to a leadership role. The story illustrates classical values throughout.

sakahpitêw 's/he tethers it [for example, a horse]'; the command or imperative form is sakahpis meaning 'tether it [animate]'.

In the mid-1880s, Big Bear said to government officials: môy ê-nôhtê-sakâpêkinikawiyân 'I don't want to be led around like a horse', a metaphorical way of saying that he did not want to be dominated by the government. This was infamously mistranslated as 'the rope about my neck' and so many assumed he was referring to hanging; a mistranslation that has cost us all a great deal. The Cree stem sakâpêkin denotes the action of controlling or guiding (a horse) by a rope or leather line. It combines sak- 'hold, attach, adhere' with -âpêk- 'rope or line', and finishing it off with -(i)n, which indicates action by the hand.

sakahpitêw can also mean 'it [inanimate] is tethered' and may have connotations of pulling because of the -pit ending (consider ocipita 'pull it'), but -ahpit usually functions together to refer to tying (for example, nîswahpitêw 's/he ties two together').

sakahpêkin is formed from sakahp- *plus* -êk- *plus* -in, with the last element referring to action by the hand. The actor or "doer" of the action uses the hand to lead someone around by rope. sîhtahpitêw can also be used relative to the act of tethering; it means 'tie tightly'; sîht- is 'tight'.

kawisimo 'go to bed'. This word is used also in the Battlefords area. My son's mother, Christine, says "kawisimo" to our son, Cody, at bedtime. This is an example of how you can begin to incorporate the Cree words that you know into daily life. There is not going to be a magical day when you suddenly become fluent; we move through the language sound by sound, and word by word.

otêma through the text of this particular story, it means 'his/her horse'. This is the same word that was traditionally used for 'his/her dog', and many assume it is a changed form of atim 'dog'.

wawêyî- 'to get ready; to make preparations'. Today, you might say, "kiwawêyîn cî?" "'are you ready?'" at the start of the day, when you and your children are heading out the door. However, in the more classical form of this story, it was used in terms of getting ready for warfare and combat, yet another example of how the dynamic Cree language takes old ideas and merges them into new situations.

spacinâsihk (ellided form of ispacinâsihk) It is rare for Bloomfield to drop initial vowels, so perhaps this is a typo, but occasionally a short /i/ is lost at the beginning of words before sC (s-consonant) clusters like the /sp/ here. The stem is ispatinaw 'hill' *plus* the -is diminutive (changing /t/ to [c] ispacinâs) and -ihk locative. Note for those who want to read Bloomfield's Cree text collections: Bloomfield originally wrote the /c/ as <ts>, so it can sometimes be difficult to tell whether he means /c/ or a contraction of /tis/ becoming <ts>.

ê-pimi-âmaciwêtâcimot 's/he crawls up a hill' or 'to crawl along upward'. Once again, note the present tense of the verb (unmarked in comparison to the past tense), which is common in classical Cree storytelling. There is a philosophical idea here, I think: the idea that the storytelling has a reality in the present moment. The stems are: pimi-, which implies something occurring in succession, in an order, toward a goal or end; âmaciwê 'to move upward'; and -tâcimo 'to crawl'. A related word is âmaciwêpicikan 'escalator'. Here, âmaciwê- is combined with –pit, which means 'action by pulling', and –kan 'thing', to form 'the thing that pulls upward'. Another related word is the name for Stanley Mission— âmaciwêspimowinihk, which refers to a high cliff where people would shoot arrows over to determine future events/possibilities (for example, the result of the arrow shooting) or simply as a test of strength. pimowin is 'shooting arrows'. The word is pronounced as âmaciwîspimowinihk in Woods Cree.

êkosi namôya kiwîcêwâkaninaw 'clearly he is not one of our comrades'. êkosi 'that's it' could be like êkosi *folks* 'that's all folks'. I think you could also use this term as it is used in this story, to note 'an obvious state of affairs'. wîcêwâkan is 'friend, companion, someone who goes with you' (in the context of this story, it refers to someone in a war party). ki- -inaw denotes 'our' (inclusive—mine and yours).

kiwî-pâskisotin 'I will shoot you'. Perhaps not the friendliest phrase from the "good old days before colonialism."

tihtipipayiho 'to roll'. I once heard my friend, the late Edward Caisse, use tihtipi-oyâkan for 'UFO'; literally, 'a rolling plate'. The -payi (-pathi, -pani) stem here is interesting and has layers of meaning. It implies a sudden movement, movement in general, and a transformation of a state of affairs. One could say that the person is 'transforming into a rolling state of being'. Remember that there is another stem for shape-shifting, which is kwêskîmo. tihtipipayiho is completed with two more meaningful elements from the amazing arsenal of Cree word structure. -h is a causative implying that the action is made to happen, while the -o ending implies that the actor or causer and the rolling object are one and the same. One literally throws oneself to roll.

DAY 39

MECHANICAL THINGS

I grew up in a very male household. One could say in Cree ê-kî-nâpê-ohpikihikawiyân 'I was raised by men'. In this upbringing, I remember my late father and my uncle, the late Burton Vandall, were always tinkering with things and fixing things. They truly loved doing these things and almost always did so without using manuals and always while speaking Cree. I think the existence of terminology for mechanical things demonstrates the dynamic nature of the Cree language.

sîhtaskêhikâkan 'screwdriver'; literally, 'the instrument that makes something tighter'. pîmahikan, literally, 'the thing with which you twist something', is another word for screwdriver.

pîmastahikan 'wrench'. Other forms that have been recorded for wrench are pîminikan 'thing you twist by hand' and âpahôstêhikan 'thing you unwind with'. Note: a variant of our main entry, pîmastêhikan has also been used, in a different context, to refer to a spinning wheel, for spinning wool into yarn.

sôhkêpocikan 'chainsaw'. Another word that has been used for chainsaw is âmow (literally, 'a bee', referring to the sound it makes). I heard this one from the late Edward Caisse, years ago.

wâsakâpayîs 'tire', referring to the circular motion of the tire.

nanâpacihtâ 'to repair something' (can refer to mechanical repairs).

nanâpacihtâwikamik 'garage'.

askihkos 'engine'; literally, 'little pail' or 'little kettle', hearkening back to the steam engines on trains, tractors, and other farm machines. They had a big kettle-like structure for creating the steam power, hence askihkos, or askihkohkân 'kettle-like thing' (remember -hkân from Day 25!).

pîwâpiskowiyinîs Cree slang for 'welder', a 'metal man'. This word might also work for the Tin Man in *The Wizard of Oz*, or maybe a heavy metal musician.

otâpânâskwa kâ-mîsahwât 'mechanic' or 'one who repairs cars'.

otâpânâskwa kâ-âpahôstinikêw 'mechanic', an alternative suggestion.

pawahikê- 'to combine' (a crop, for example). So use a combine (pawahikan) on the crops.

akohkasikê- 'to weld'. I wanted to share this final word for a variety of reasons. This is the word that my father and uncles used for welding. My understanding is that it literally means 'cooking or baking something together'. This is another example of the way in which Crees use perfectly understandable words and verbs to explain new technology.

I remember once when they were welding, they spoke of our grandfather Gabriel Vandall, who received about twenty medals in combat. He was one of the first men to land at Juno Beach on D-Day. Once on shore, the Canadians realized that they were taking heavy fire from the German guns. Our mosôm thought it would be a good idea to weld extra pieces of metal to the tanks to give them more protection. I don't think there is any record in history books of the deeds of our mosôm, this Cree-Métis man who thought of making the armour of the tanks stronger.

Stories are important, I think, for learning words—they give them a context.

DAY 40

TREATY FOUR
LEADERS

When I was a boy, I used to travel with my late mosôm John R. McLeod. He was chosen to be the chair of the Treaty Six Centennial in 1976. I have always had a deep interest in Treaties and, of course, in the leaders.

Following is a list of some of the leaders at the time of the signing of Treaty Four. Remember, despite what some history books note, the pipestem was used to enter into the Treaty (oral history—the late Gabriel Crow Buffalo). While the list contains mostly male leaders at the time, it should be remembered that Indigenous women played a key role in the deliberations. Oral histories and also Band Treaty paylists would be good places to start researching and gathering the names of these women.

wâpi-mostosis 'White Calf'.

acâhkosa k-ôtakohpit 'Starblanket'; literally, 'he has the stars for a blanket', son of White Calf.

okinîs 'Rose-hip'.

paškwâ 'The Prairie' (brother of okinîs).

kâ-kisîwêw piyêsiw 'Loud Voice' (kâ-kišîwê in Saulteaux).

kâ-awâsis 'The Child' (kwîwîsêns in Saulteaux). This is Cowessess.

kaskitêwi-maskwa-maskosis 'Little Black Bear'.

kâ-nahahcâpîw 'The One who Readies the Bow' (father of pîhpîkisîs).

kîsikâw-acâhkos 'Day Star' (from the Touchwood Hills area).

kawâhkatos 'Lean Man' (from the Touchwood Hills area).

omîmî 'Pidgeon' (in Saulteaux); he was named Gabriel Côté in English.

kîhšikôns 'Keeseekoose' or 'Little Sky' in Saulteaux (kîsikos in Cree).

ocâpahowês 'The One who Unties [the Rope]' (son of kâ-kisîwêw piyêsiw).

ahki-ahkiwênsî 'Earth Elder' from Sakimay; there is a well-known book about him, called *Earth Elder Stories*.

kâ-ošawâstêk 'Orange Light' (Hilda Pelletier), a well-known keeper of traditional knowledge (daughter of Earth Elder).

DAY 41

HORSES (PART 2)

In May 2011 I had the fortune of going out to Blackfoot Crossing for the mounting of the retrospective James Henderson exhibition. While there, our host, Treffery Deerfoot, took us to the herd of old-style horses on the reserve. These horses are of the same type that would have existed in the pre-reserve period. They are the kind of horses that the old Crees would have drawn upon to achieve their glory and honour.

Here are terms collected by David Mandelbaum in the 1930s (from *The Plains Cree*, p. 65). Mandelbaum collected these words at a time when the Plains Cree people were being repressed, and they were very eager to share stories and insights with Mandelbaum. An important gathering was held in 1975 in Fort Qu'Appelle, where Cree kêhtê-ayak met with Mandelbaum to review what he had compiled. Many of the Cree who gathered were the daughters and sons and, in some cases, grandchildren, of those who had been interviewed. I have watched the original tapes of this gathering, and I recall how Mandelbaum was very kind and was open to hearing the limitations of his study. He struck me as a man who was genuinely interested in Cree people and wanted to record some elements of our culture and language.

These are descriptions for horses collected by Mandelbaum, and the initial translations in double quotes are his originals. We have, however, attempted to regularize his Cree spelling to today's Standard Roman Orthography.

wâpastim "gray or white"; literally, 'white horse'.

masinâsowatim "pinto"; literally, a 'coloured horse' or one with very interesting colour. I think that this could be used for the six hundred beautiful wild horses we saw at Blackfoot Crossing.

osâwihtawakay "yellow ears".

kakaskitêwihtawakay "black ears".

wiyîpâpastim "dark gray". To me this word sounds like earth being moved and thrown about—which matches perfectly with the colour the word describes.

wâpanôskâyow "silver tail". This one is particularly problematic. It was written as "wapanuskago", but the 'g' is almostly certainly a typo, and this only adds to the obscurity of the derivation of this name.

nîpênâkowês "iron grey". This appears to describe a 'dark grey' like the pitch-dark night (nîpê-), therefore 'iron grey'. The other elements are then likely -nâkw-, indicating 'appearance', and -awê, referring to the horse's 'hide'.

kaskitêwastim "black"; literally, 'black horse'.

wâpihkwêwastim "bald face"; literally, 'white-faced horse'.

wiyîpastim "brown"; literally, 'brown or dirty horse'.

mihkwawêwatim "bay"; literally, 'red-coated horse'.

âpakosîsi-pîway "mouse-coloured": pîway 'fur, coat, or plumage'.

wâwâskêsiwi-pîway "buckskin"; literally, 'elk-coated'. These last two (and many others here) are interesting examples of Cree metaphor—using one instance of colour to describe another one. Note: the Blackfoot call horses 'Elk Dogs'.

osâwasiskîwi-pîway "yellow mud".

osâwastim "sorrel"; literally, 'yellow horse'.

wânokawês "chestnut". The derivation for this word is uncertain.

mîhyawêwastim "shaggy haired".

sîsîkiyawastim "roan" (grey and brown). Note: Mandelbaum also lists wâpohkatim as roan.

pâhpâhtêwastim "dappled". pâhpâhtêw- refers to large spots.

wâpinâkwatay "white spot on belly". And presumably then kaskitênâkwatay would be 'black spot on belly'; osâwinâkwatay, 'yellow spot on belly'; and so on. If so, the elements here are wâpi- 'white', -nâkw- 'appearance', and -atay 'belly'.

wâpiskisôkan "white hindquarters, black markings, small tail": wâpisk- 'white'; -sôkan 'rump, buttocks'.

kakaskitêw "gray, dark hindquarters".

Many of the wild horses I saw at Blackfoot Crossing fit these descriptions. Also, the names that include atim or -astim could be, and in some cases certainly were, used to refer to both dogs and horses.

POWWOW (PART 1)

Of course, for many Cree people (and other Indigenous Nations), powwow is a key part of many people's lives. I recall in the 1970s, I would travel with nimosômipan to many, particularly in the North Battleford area. I remember nimosômipan would make bannock for about three days before the powwows, and he would put it in a great container and give it to people. I remember the open air of those long trips, and the way people were always visiting and laughing. I remember powwows as being a place where Indian culture was valued, and where kêhtê-ayak were held in high honour. As such, I thought it would be worthwhile to start to gather some of the terminology related to powwow.

pwâtisimo 'dance powwow'; literally, 'dance the Sioux/Dakota dance'.

wawikisimo 'fancy dance'. Jean Okimâsis notes, "It sounds like someone is dancing while bending or in a bent position."

kayâsisimowin 'traditional dancing'.

maskihkîwisimowin 'jingle-dress dancing'; literally, 'the medicine dance'.

pîhtikwêsimowin 'grand entry'. This can also refer to the dance performed when chiefs were inducted and an honour song was sung.

nîmihitowikamik 'powwow arbour'; ita kâ-pwâtisimohk literally means 'where powwow dancing occurs'.

pihêwisimowin 'chicken dance'. The old Cree dance of the okihcitâwak.

pwâtisimoskanaw 'powwow trail'.

pakamânâhtik 'drum stick' (for singing).

wâhkôhtowin 'powwow politics' (cah!).

âpihtâw-âpihtâw '50/50'. Okay, maybe just âh-âpihtâw.

âh-âhtapi 'powwow group hopping'; literally, 'keep changing your seat'.

apiscisimowin 'tiny-tot dance'.

ê-yahkatâmohk 'a start up' (in powwow singing).

HOW SWEETGRASS BECAME CHIEF (PART 5)
FROM *PLAINS CREE TEXTS*

Today we continue studying the vocabulary of the story as told by Simon Mimikwas. These narratives collected by Bloomfield have provided such an important bank of language and stories for us to draw upon as we retrieve our language with great effort and enthusiasm.

misahkamik ayisiyiniwa 'great many people'. As this is an obviative form (see the -a ending on ayisiyiniw), it refers to a group of people other than those involved in the main part of the story.

waskâmo 'to flee' (in the context of warfare); tapasî is another stem meaning 'to flee'. It would be interesting to determine the difference between these two terms. Is waskâmo simply a classical stem?

âsowahamwak sîpîsis 'they cross the creek'. Note: once again, the story was written in the present tense (but the events really occurred in the past). Part of my work with *Plains Cree Texts* will be to ensure the translation of the whole body of the text/narratives into Cree is in the present tense. By doing so, we will better capture the intention of the Cree storytellers.

sêkopayihow 'he hides': sêko- 'go underneath'; the complex ending -payiho provides the implication of 'moving oneself suddenly'. Together they result in the sense of "hide" within the context of warfare.

sêskâmo 'to flee into the woods'.

mâhi-kôkî 'to dive downstream'.

mêniskihkê 'to make trenches and earthworks'. This is mênisk 'trench, earthwork' *plus* -ihkê (compare with -(i)hkân: *see* Day 25). This is a different stem from mônahikê 'dig, mine', a stem used in another narrative in *Plains Cree Texts*.

okimâwi 'to be a chief'.

kîskihkomân 'Cutknife' or, more correctly, 'Broken Knife'. He is initially identified as Blackfoot but later identified as sâsîw (Sarcee, Tsuu T'ina).

wîhkwêskaw 'head someone off, surround someone'.

nôtinikê 'to fight'. kihci-nôtinikêwin means 'First World War'. The addition of kihci- to the stem demonstrates how the scale of that war changed their conception of warfare from classical times.

wayacâwî 'stand ready to run, escape' (for example, during combat).

têpwê 'to make a war whoop'; it usually just means 'to yell, to call out'. Black Powder, Big Bear's father, was in a band whose Cree leader was called 'He Who Gives a War Whoop'.

câpês The name of a Cree involved in the battle. I know this probably means 'Little Man' because câpês was the name of the late Charlie Burns's older brother.

wasakâw-awâsis 'Clawchild'. The name of a Cree involved in the battle.

manihkomânêk! 'get your knives ready!' or 'take the knives!'.

sâkowê 'to make a loud sound' during combat instructions or communication to fellow combatants. This has also been translated as giving a 'war whoop' as well as to 'yell' or 'shout'. Probably one had to shout commands loudly during combat.

manis(w) 'to take someone's scalp'; literally, 'to cut someone'. This can also be used for performing surgery today.

otinamwak ostikwân 'they take a scalp'; literally, 'they take a head'.

mêscih 'to eliminate someone'. In the context of this story, it means to eliminate the enemy. It's a collective verb.

sîsîpistikwân 'Duck Head', the one Blackfoot who dives in the river in the story.

kâh-kâsôw 'he just hid in the tree'. He was the one Blackfoot who survived the battle.

DAY 44

POWWOW (PART 2)

There are so many words associated with powwow that I thought I would compile at least one more list. Of course, there are many more words to gather, but I hope this will be a good start.

kâ-ohpî-kâhkâkiw 'crow hop'. kâhkâkiwisimowin 'raven dance'. Note that the Indigenous nation of the Crow in Cree is actually 'raven'.

otêpwêstamâkêw 'MC'; kihci-opîkiskwêw 'great speaker'. Tyrone Tootoosis also confirmed that otêpwêstamâkêw has its origins in the camp crier.

kahkiyaw awiyak 'intertribal'; literally, 'everyone'. Another term for intertribal is kahkiyaw ê-nîmihitohk.

nîmihito-ayiwinisa 'regalia'; literally, 'dancing clothes'.

î-sôhkanitahk 'fast beat' (Woods Cree).

î-papiyâhtikihtâkwahk 'slow beat' (Woods Cree). Plains Cree would be ê-papêyâhtakihtâkwahk.

osêskicês 'roach'; also sêskicês.

mâskikanâpisk 'breastplate'.

kâpêsi 'to camp'.

kiyokê 'to visit'.

nîmihito-okimâskwêsis 'Powwow Princess'.

SWEETGRASS AS A YOUNG MAN (PART 1)

FROM *PLAINS CREE TEXTS*

The rich narrative legacy provided by the kêhtê-ayak recorded by Leonard Bloomfield give us an insight into the early life of wîhkasko-kisêyin. By knowing these details of his life, we can better understand the forces that shaped his concepts of leadership, and which in turn helped shape the diplomatic history of the Cree Nation. The terms below are from the story as told by kâ-kîsikâw-pîhtokêw (Coming Day).

kêkâ-mitâtaht ê-ihtasicik 'They numbered nine' (in a war party).

sipwêhtê 'to leave by foot'. This story provides evidence of the fact that the Cree were often 'horse poor'.

wiyanih- 'skin and cut up [something animate]' as in 'dress a slaughtered animal'—in this context, a buffalo; a modified stem would be needed to refer to skinning in general.

kaskikwâta 'sew [something]', 'mend [something] by sewing', for example, moccasins.

ê-wî-kakwê-wâpamât ayahciyiniwa 'he tries to see the Blackfoot'. An interesting expression used to talk about Sweetgrass's desire to travel to the land of the Blackfoot—to the territory of the Blackfoot. The statement and expression shows that warfare was not simply about killing but also curiosity.

asawâpi 'look out' (as in scouting).

ê-pitihkwêyik 'it makes a thudding sound'; this is the same stem used in nipiy kâ-pitihkwêk (the name of Sounding Lake).

ê-ispatinâyik 'the land rises; there is a hill': isp- 'high'; ispatinâ-'to be a hill'.

sâkêwê- 'to come into view'. This is also used to refer to the sun when it rises.

mostos used for 'buffalo'; today 'buffalo' is usually paskwâ-mostos and mostos by itself usually just means 'cow'.

ê-pê-nawaswâtâyit ôhi mostoswa 'they came chasing the buffalo'. The obviative form on the verb indicates that this is a secondary topic, not the main topic of the story.

apisîs ê-sakâsiyik 'small clump of trees'.

acosisa ê-tahkonahk 'he carried his arrows'.

ê-tahkonamiyit pâskisikan 'he carries a gun'.

mahti kisiwâk kita-ayât 'I will draw him in close' (in the context of combat); literally, 'may it be that he will draw near'.

ê-askôkot 'someone is following/pursuing him'.

wâyinopit- 'to turn back [on a horse]'. The -pit element, which always has to do with pulling, indicates that this refers to the motion on the reins. The command form would be wâyinopis.

nîhciwêpahw- 'to knock someone down or off of [something]'; here, the context implies 'off of a horse'.

ê-kimotamawâcik otêmiyiwa 'they stole their horses'. The obviation on -têm- 'horse(s)' indicates they were not stealing their own horses.

DAY 46

HOUSEHOLD ITEMS

Today's terms can be used to describe everyday household items, once again demonstrating the adaptability of the Cree language.

kisîpêkinikâkan, kisîpêkinikêpayîs, kisîpêkini-mahkahk, *or* kisîpêkinikêwi-mahkahk all four terms are for 'washer' or 'washing machine'. mahkahk means 'tub' here but can also be a 'barrel'.

pastêpicikan, pâhkwastêwinikan 'dryer'.

kâspihkasikan 'toaster'; literally, 'the thing that bakes it crispy'.

kêsiskâwihkasikan 'microwave'; also kisîhkasikan—both imply something that cooks quickly.

napwên 'frying pan' (from a French loan word); there was an Old Man from Sandy Lake called napwên.

sâsâpiskisikan, sâsêskihkwân, sêsêskihkwân 'frying pan'.

askihkos 'pail, bucket, or kettle'. This can also means 'engine'—after the old steam engines that needed a large, kettle-like container for the water.

âstawêpita 'turn off the light'.

wâsênamân 'window'.

wâsaskotêpayihcikan 'electricity, power'; although some simply use iskotêw 'fire' for electricity.

DAY 47

SONGS TO KILL
A WÎHTIKOW

The event Cree Stories, held in Winnipeg in 2011, got me thinking about Cree poetic words. Here are some poetic words/phrases from my first book of poetry, *Songs to Kill a Wîhtikow*. I used the metaphor of wîhtikow to articulate the darkness I have faced in my life. My philosophy is simple: if we are to overcome hardship, then we have to understand and name the darkness and pain that we have felt.

Here are some words and phrases, some of which I coined.

kisêyiniwak ê-wâsakâmapicik 'Old Men sat in a circle'.

sâh-sîhcisiwak 'crowded seating' (to sit tightly packed together).

ê-sâh-sâkiniskêpayihot 'he kept showing his hidden hand quickly'.

kâ-askîwikâpawit 'standing earth'.

ê-sîpi-kiskisiyân 'I stretch my memory'.

aya, ânisko-âcimocik ê-kistawêcik 'they connected through speaking, echoes'.

kapê ê-yôskipayik 'forever moving softly'.

kâ-pawâtahk nipiy 'dreaming water'.

sâpwâstan 'wind blowing through'.

askîhk ohci 'from the earth'.

itê ê-mamâhtâwisiyahk 'where we tap into the powers of the universe' (a metaphorical word to describe physical intimacy).

ya-yôskisin 'to lay down very gently'.

kâ-yôskitonêt 'the softness of her/his lips'.

nimamâhtâwipêsinin kiyawihk ohci 'I lay in the divinity of the water of your body'.

DAY 48

FLOWERS

When I think of flowers, I often think of the very colourful skirts that kôhkominawak 'our grandmothers' often had when I was growing up in the 1970s. Their colours were so vibrant and were in contrast to the rubbers and moccasins that they also wore. Of course, many of these flowers, like kôhkominawak, are sources of medicine, and help keep our beings whole. These wâpakwaniya also help fill our traditional territories with beautiful colours.

wâpakwaniy/wâpikwaniy 'flower'; both spellings are common, as are the alternate pronunciations. Also, the /wa/ sequence after the /k/ often gets pronounced as an [o], and so wâpakoniy/wâpikoniy also occur. Shorter versions like âpikwaniy/pikwaniy/-kwaniy, etc., may occur in compounds.

osâwâpikwanîs 'dandelion'; literally, the 'little yellow flower'. pîsim-wâpikwaniy is also 'dandelion'; literally, 'sun flower'. It is interesting that some people think of these flowers as weeds but our people used the plant for maskihkiy 'medicine'.

wâpakwaniy-mîkisistahikêwin 'floral beadwork'.

yôskahtêpakwa 'tiger lily'. Dorothy Thunder and okâwiya had this word. yôsk- is usually 'soft' and -pakwa is a plural referring to plants in general. We're not certain of the derivation of the middle section.

mihkokwaniy 'rose'; but this implies that it is a red rose—it literally means 'red flower'.

okiniy 'rosehip'. Remember that the southern leader okinîs was the brother of paskwâ. nôhkom, the late Ida McLeod, also wrote a series of books with the title of okinîs (as the name of a girl).

waskatamiw 'yellow pond lily'.

wâpakwanî- 'to have flowers'; for example, ê-wâpikwanît, in reference to an animate plant.

nanâtohkwâpakwanî- 'to have variously coloured flowers'.

wâpiskâpakwanîs 'a little white flower'.

pêyakwaskokâpawiw 'it stands as one blade or stem'.

pêyak nîpîs 'one little leaf' (a petal). paskêkin means 'it grows separately/off to the side/as an offshoot'; pahki-wâpakwaniy is 'part of a flower'.

DAY 49

INTERACTING WITH OUR CHILDREN (PART 1)

Jacqueline Anaquod asked if I could put together a word list for interacting with our children on a practical, daily basis. Personally, I think that passing our language on to children holds the future of our language. If we can successfully engage our children, and those osk-âyak 'young beings' of the coming generations, then our language, like a seed, will find a place to grow and to extend into the future. Today, we will look at practical words to use when engaging with our children, who I remember hearing many times are on loan to us from the Creator.

kisâkihitin 'I love you'.

pêyâhtik 'be careful' (also pêyâhtak).

wâniskâ, pê-wâpan ôma 'wake up, the dawn has come'. I remember one time kâ-miywâsik (Ernest Tootoosis) said this one—he stressed the need to wake children up gently.

kiyipa 'hurry up'. Sounds like [KEE puh].

kawisimo 'go to bed, go to sleep'.

kipaha iskwâhtêm 'close the door'.

yôhtêna iskwâhtêm 'open the door'.

mahti miyin anima 'please give me that, pass me that'.

mîciso 'eat'.

kikîspon cî? 'are you full?'.

cêskwa 'wait'.

pêhin 'wait for me'.

âstam 'come here'.

wîcikâpawîstamawin 'stand by me, stand with me'.

atamiskaw 'shake his/her hand'.

kâsîyâkanê 'wash the dishes'.

kisîpêkinikê 'do the laundry'.

100 DAYS OF CREE

DAY 50

SEWING/HIDES

An important component of traditional Cree culture is the making of hides and sewing. Certainly, this aspect of our culture allowed us to survive in the world and have clothing to keep our bodies warm. Hides also allowed us to create beautiful objects of art. The skills of women, and of course men, too, in this regard, were highly valued, and continue to be valued today.

kaskikwâsowin 'sewing'.

nanâtohkokwâsow 'she sews various materials together; s/he sews patchwork blankets; s/he quilts'.

asapâp 'thread'.

tâpisaha 'thread it' (for example, the needle).

pahkêkin 'leather'.

mâtahikan 'hide scraper'.

mihkipitamowin 'fleshing [hides]'. Note: we're not absolutely sure we've represented this one correctly. mihkihkwan is a 'flesher' and mihkita is 'flesh it', so mihkitamowin should also be 'the act of fleshing'.

pahkêkinohkêwin 'preparing hides'.

kaskikwâsopayihcikan 'sewing machine'.

pahkêkinwêyâpiya 'leather fringes'. Another word for fringes is simply yîwêsikan 'something cut to hang loosely'.

DAY 51

INTERACTING WITH OUR CHILDREN (PART 2)

Here are some more practical things to say to kids. I encourage people to use all of the Cree words they have. Every word you say to your children plants little "memory seeds" in their minds, which can grow in the future. Every little bit we can do to encourage them to learn and practice the language will help to ensure its survival.

kimosôm 'your grandfather'. Remember not all mosômak 'grandfathers' are biological grandfathers. Our open kinship system is probably one of the reasons our culture persists, as these relationships are very powerful; nimosôm is 'my grandfather'.

kôhkom 'your grandmother'. Remember we don't have great-aunts in Cree, we just say nôhkom 'my grandmother'.

mahti nêhiyawê 'speak Cree'; the mahti softens it up so that it does not seem so abrupt.

kakwê-nêhiyawê 'try to speak Cree'.

kakwê-nêhiyawêmototawin 'try to speak Cree to me'.

pimipahtâ 'run'.

taskamohtê 'walk across'. And taskamohtêtân is 'let's walk across' (a street, for example).

ê-wî-naskwênitân 'I'm going to pick you up' (that is, provide you with a ride); naskwên- is one verb stem indicating to pick someone up; although it also implies catching someone as they go by.

nakiskâtotân [*insert number*] **tipahikan ispayiki** 'let's meet at [X] o'clock': nakiskaw 'to meet someone'; -ito is the reciprocal that makes the verb refer to 'each other'; -tân 'let's' (you and me).

kiya 'you'. (kîtha, kîna are Woods and Swampy dialectal variations.)

niya 'I, me'. (nîtha, nîna are Woods and Swampy dialectal variations.)

iskonikanihk cî ê-nôhtê-itâcihoyan? *or* **ê-nôhtê-pimohtêhoyan cî iskonikanihk isi?** 'Do you want to travel to the reserve?'. nôhtê-is 'want', but you need a verb to go with it; you can't just say it by itself. pimâciho and pimohtêho are both stems for 'travel'; itâciho means 'travel [somewhere]'; and -yan makes the verb refer to 'you'.

ê-nitawêyihtaman cî ôma? 'Do you want this?'.

DAY 52

DOGS

Dogs played a major role in Cree culture. Once again, I do not want to overstep my bounds, but here a little bit of historical and cultural context is useful. In the springtime, in the territory of my relatives from Sandy Lake, the people would gather and have a dog feast. During this time, they would also harvest the sap from the birch trees.

Before horses, dogs were absolutely essential for moving things and camps. Women owned these dogs, and things did change when Crees acquired the horses (at least, on the plains). Within Cree culture, as I understand it, dogs were also seen as protectors of people in a spiritual sense. They were considered to absorb negative energies for people, and they were deeply cared for. In the old days, the dogs were not allowed in the mîkiwâhpa 'tipis'. The late Charlie Burns told me that part. Today, we let our dogs into our houses. Despite this difference, I think we still value them a great deal today.

atim 'dog'.

acimosis 'puppy'.

sâsinikonastimwê 'pet one's dog(s)'.

simâkanis-atim 'German shepherd'.

tipwêstikwân-acimosis 'poodle'; literally, 'curly-hair dog'.

atimo-kîmwês 'dog whisperer' (cah! I made this one up): atimo-pertaining to 'dog'; kîmwê- 'whisper'.

yâpêwatim 'pitbull' (I coined this as well): yâpêw 'bull, bull moose'; atim 'dog'.

atimotâpânêyâpiya 'dog harness'.

takahkatim 'good dog'.

otâpahâkan 'a pack dog'; also 'a draft horse'.

yêhêsi 'to pant from the heat'; also yêyêsi.

atimotâpânâsk 'dogsled'.

DAY 53

HORSES (PART 3)

Today, we continue to look at horse terms. Undoubtedly, there are many more words and phrases that we could gather, given the historical importance of the horse to Plains Cree culture.

ta-papâmâpêkinak misatim 'for me to lead a horse about'.

ay-âsowakâmi-têhtapit 's/he crosses a river on a horse'.

kâ-taskam-têhtapiyân sîpiy 'I cross the river on a horse'.

misatimosoy 'horse tail'.

nôsêstim 'female horse'. Note: nôsê- is a useful add-on in Cree because it can be put ahead of many noun stems to show the being in question is a female (for example, nôsê-amisk is 'a female beaver').

misatimokamik 'horse barn'.

kiskisis 'mare'.

mêstakaya 'mane' (or 'hair').

nâpêstim 'male horse, stud horse'; this word has certain connotations sometimes used to describe human males (nudge, nudge, wink, wink).

wâyisitêhikan 'horseshoe'.

pêtastimwê 'to bring horses'.

mihcêtastimwê 'to have many horses'.

DAY 54

FURNITURE

I remember hearing from my friend Jerry Fineday that his câpân, Fineday, did not like to sit on furniture. Rather, Fineday liked to sit on the floor when he would tell stories, and people from all over would gather to hear him. I have also heard about others who thought sitting in our modern chairs was strange, and not to their taste. But furniture has become part of our lives today.

kâ-kinwâk têhtapiwin 'couch'; literally, 'the chair which is long'.

kâ-nistokâtêk 'stool'; literally, 'the thing that has three legs'.

sâkihito-têhtapiwin 'loveseat'.

kihtimikanêw-têhtapiwin 'recliner; La-Z-Boy'.

kâ-ahkwêhtawastêki nipêwina 'bunk beds'; literally, 'the beds that are stacked on each other'.

nipêwin 'bed'.

nipêwinis 'cot' (a little bed).

wâsaskotêhikan 'lamp'.

okimâw-têhtapiwin 'chief chair'. I am not sure if this is the right term in Cree, but it refers to the ornate chairs that well-respected chiefs would sometimes sit in in the old days. They had a lot of white on them, as well as designs. kihc-ôkimâwapiwin has been used as a translation for 'throne'.

pwâtisimo-têhtapiwin 'powwow chair'.

akocikan 'cupboard'; literally, 'the thing that you hang things on'.

mîcisowinâhtik 'table'; literally, 'the thing made of wood that you eat on'; -âhtik is the stem for 'wood/made of wood'.

tâpasinahikêwinâhtik 'drawing table'.

nahastâso 'make the bed'.

DAY 55

COLOURS

Colours are an interesting topic in Cree, and there is a great deal of regional variation in describing them. As my friend Darren Okemaysim notes, many of the terms for colours are metaphors based on other things—Cree is a deeply and profoundly poetic language. Here is how Darren says it: "Colours in Cree can be etymologically sourced back to natural elements of kikâwînaw askiy 'Mother Earth' and thus can corroborate Cree values and perspectives within the language. Etymology in linguistics can be defined as the 'history, evolution, or origin of words.'"

The search for colour terms is an example of how we can learn about Cree meanings by drawing upon Anishinaabemowin terms. (A million miigs to Shirley Williams from downtown wiikwemekong for helping out with these terms!) Note that there is an interesting cluster of terms in Cree and Anishinaabemowin relating to the colours for brown, orange, and yellow.

mihkwâw 'it is red' (inanimate); mihkosiw 'it is red' (animate). Etymology: mihko 'blood'.

sîpihkwâw 'it is blue' (inanimate); sîpihkosiw 'it is blue' (animate). Etymology: sîpiy 'river'.

wâpiskâw 'it is white' (inanimate); wâpiskisiw 'it is white' (animate). Etymology: wâpisiw 'swan'. Also, the root /wâp-/ is associated with such things as 'white' (consider the prenoun wâpi- in wâpi-maskwa 'White Bear'), 'light', and 'vision' (for example, the verb wâpi 'to see', and namôya niwâpin 'I am blind'). This root can also be extended as /wâpisk-/, the stem from which the colour terms are derived and the base of another prenoun wâpiski-, as in wâpiski-mîmêw 'white dove'.

osâwâw 'it is orange' (inanimate); osâwisiw 'it is orange' (animate). Etymology: osâwaskosiy 'yellow grass'. Note: some speakers, such as Randy Morin and Karen Chamakese, name orange as osâwi-mihkwâw (which translates as 'yellow-red'), and for them osâwaw means 'it is yellow'. The fruit 'orange' is called osâwâs in many locations. Chris Hunter named atisonâkosiw as the basic stem for 'orange'. He said it referred to the 'sky colour before the sun sets', and it can also mean 'tan' or 'brown'; literally, 'it appears tanned'.

In Anishinaabemowin, the word for 'orange' is (o) zaawmingaanwaande. Once again, you have the stem -aande 'to be coloured'. The zaaw- is a reduced form of ozaaw-, which sometimes means 'yellow' in Anishinaabemowin. The stem -mingaanw-modifies the 'yellow' to mean 'orange'. When we were talking about this colour, I asked Shirley Williams about the word for copper. When I was a child, I loved looking at Norval Morrisseau's paintings and I recall recognizing the stem ozaawaa (osâwâ- in Cree) in his name, which means 'Copper Thunderbird'. Copper, a material gathered by the Anishinaabeg, is ozaawaabig: the stem ozaaw- is combined with the stem -aabig, which means 'stone' or 'metal', like -âpisk in Cree. Note: 'gold' in Cree is osâwi-sôniyâw or osâwi-sôniyâwâpisk (which can also mean 'copper').

askihtakwâw 'it is green' (inanimate); askihtakosiw 'it is green' (animate)'. Etymology: askiy 'land'. Another root related to askiy in Cree is /ask-/, referring to 'fresh' or 'raw'. The stem upon which the colour terms are built combines this with /-ihtak(w)/ 'wood, board', forming askihtakw- 'fresh wood', and the prenoun askihtako- 'green'. Note: Anishinaabemowin also uses descriptions of land to represent colour: for example, ekiiyaande is formed from ekiiy- 'earth' (ahki in Saulteaux) and -aande 'the way in which it is coloured'. For the Anishinaabeg in the east, 'earth colour' means 'brown'.

kaskitêwâw 'it is black' (inanimate); kaskitêsiw 'it is black' (animate). Etymology: kaskicês 'coal or remnant of fire'.

wâpikwanîwinâkwan 'it is pink' (inanimate); wâpikwanîwinâkosiw 'it is pink' (animate). Etymology: wâpikwaniy 'flower'. Note: the metaphor here is dependent on the flower being pink, like the roses of okinîwâhtik 'the wild rose bush'.

cîpêhtakwâw 'it is grey' (inanimate); cîpêhtakosiw 'it is grey' (animate). Etymology: cîpay 'spirit, ghost'. Note: this is another colour term that relies on the metaphor of the colour of a certain type of wood /-ihtak(w)/, the dried out, grey 'ghost' or dead wood.

wîskwastêwinâkwan 'it is brown' (inanimate); wîskwastêwinâkosiw 'it is brown' (animate). Etymology: wîskwastêw 'it is smoked (tanned)'.

Randy Morin had the term wîstêpahkwênakwâw for 'brown' (inanimate). This term contains the form wîstêpahkwê-, also found in wîstêpahkwêwikamik 'a tent made of bits of old (brown) leather'. Chris Hunter, from northern Ontario, used the term kihci-osâwisiw, which means 'great orange/yellow' (animate). To add to this variation of Chris Hunter's, my uncle, the late Burton Vandall from Sandy Lake, once told me brown was kâskitê-osâwâw, which means 'dark yellow/orange' (inanimate), while clearly compounding 'black' and 'yellow'. Yet another term that has been used is wîposâwâw, combining /wîp-/ or /wiyip-/ 'dirty' with osâwâw, and so 'dirty yellow'. Many of these words show that / osâw-/ or osâwâw is a basic colour term, with various modifications indicating related shades. A relationship among terms for yellow, orange, and brown is very common in a variety of the world's languages.

nîpâmâyâtan 'it is purple' (inanimate); nîpâmâyâtisiw 'it is purple' (animate). Etymology: nîpâ-tipisk 'late into the night/purple haze of moon'. Note: the endings of these words are essentially mâyâtan and mâyâtisiw, which are the inanimate and animate verbs meaning 'ugly', such that this colour term can be translated as 'deep ugly'. There are a variety of terms for purple: for example, my friend from Onion Lake, John Quinney, used the metaphor of a bruise: ahpîhtinâkwan 'it is purple' (inanimate), and ahpîhtinâkosiw 's/he or it is purple' (animate). Yet others simply use compounds like mihko-sîpihkwâw 'it is red-blue', or sîpihko-mihkwâw 'it is blue-red'.

wâposâwâw 'it is yellow' (inanimate); wâposâwisiw 'it is yellow' (animate). Etymology: wâpos 'rabbit' (relating to fur colour during seasonal change). Note: as mentioned above, in some dialects of Cree, osâwâw by itself means 'yellow'. In comparing some of the other terms already described above, it is also clear that, although these terms certainly sound as if they contain wâpos 'rabbit', and this is an excellent way to help children remember these words, they can also be viewed as a derivation of /wâp-/ *plus* osâwâw/osâwisiw, and thus mean something like 'light osâwâw/light osâwisiw', paralleling wîposâwâw as 'dirty' or 'dark osâwâw'. Again, this fine-tuning is done in order to narrow down the meaning of /osâw-/, which can vary when applied to the great variety of shades of yellow, orange, and brown.

itasinâstêw 'it is of such a colour' (inanimate); itasinâsow 'it is of such a colour' (animate).

tânisi ê-itasinâstêk? 'what colour is it?' (inanimate); tânisi ê-itasinâsot? 'what colour is it?' (animate).

DAY 56

FORESTS

The theme for today is forests. I grew up on the James Smith Reserve—which is just at the edge of the parklands and where the heavy bush begins—and it was here that my father, Jerry McLeod, taught me many things. He left us in June 2011, and his passing brought home to me the necessity of working hard to preserve and pass on our language. We are, after all, the living present of ancestral legacy.

I have to thank my father for giving me the seeds of language and history, which have given me the foundation upon which I stand today.

sakâw 'bush'; 'woods'; 'forest'.

sakâwiyiniwak the Plains Cree name for the 'Woods/Woodland/Bush Cree'.

asiniy-nîhithawak 'Rock Cree'; another name for the Woodlands Cree (from areas of northern Saskatchewan and northern Manitoba).

kawâhtik 'fallen tree'.

watihkwan 'tree branch'; also miscikos 'stick'.

oskipêmakâw 'undergrowth'.

mahihkan 'wolf' (an important being of the forests).

maskwa 'bear' (another important being of the forests).

wayakêsk 'tree bark'.

mêstan 'inner bark'.

minahik 'pine tree'.

sôkâwâhtik 'cedar tree'; literally, 'sugar tree'. This word has also been applied to the 'sugar maple'.

waskwêtoy 'pine cone'.

sihtak 'spruce trees'; also, possibly, 'tree cover'.

nîpisiy 'willow tree'.

opâskwêyâhk 'The Pas': opâw or wapâw 'a narrows', -âskw- 'wood/tree', -êyâ a landform ending, and -hk is the locative. Arok Wolvengrey suggests that this refers to a wooded narrows, where the trees overshadow the river.

sakimêskâw 'there are lots of mosquitos'.

mistikoskâw 'wooded area'; literally, 'there are lots of trees'.

mistikokamik 'log cabin'. We have various words for cabin: wâskahikanis 'little house' (*see* Day 16 for the root meaning of the word); kapêsiwikamikos 'little shelter for camping or resting' (remember the stem -kamikos can sometimes be rendered as 'room': *see* Day 22); napakikamik refers to a 'flat-roofed structure' with a sod roof (sometimes also used for a 'wall tent').

sêskisi- 'to walk into the woods'; ê-papâmisakâwêt 's/he walks in the woods'.

DAY 57

ART TERMS (PART I)

I collected the following terms a kayâs long time ago in the 1990s. They were part of those published in an education guide for the Mendel Art Gallery, in Saskatoon, and also in the newsletter of the Cree Language Retention Committee, edited by Arok Wolvengrey. I enjoyed the challenge of trying to think of how to say various art terms in Cree. I think it helps to try to learn a vocabulary of words for things that are important to you. It's an enjoyable way to build up your skill level.

pâskihcikâtêw ta-itwêstamâkêhk 'abstract'; literally, 'it is open to interpretation'.

tâpasinahikêwikamik 'art gallery'; literally, 'drawing building'.

nâwayihk 'background'; literally, 'in the back'.

wâwiyêyâw 'circle'.

kâ-mâwacihtâhk 'collection'; literally, 'that which is collected'.

kâ-isi-astêk 'composition'; literally, 'how it is situated'.

okanawêyihcikêw 'curator'; literally, 'one who takes care of things'; also, okanawâpahcikêw 'one who looks after things'.

kâ-iskonâkwahk 'horizon'; literally, 'what is left in appearance'; a metaphor to discuss a horizon line.

askiy kâ-tâpasinahamihk 'landscape (painting/drawing)'; literally, 'when the earth is drawn'.

pimiy kâ-ohci-masinipêhikâkêhk 'oil painting; painting with oil'.

kâ-tâpasinahoht ayisiyiniw 'portrait'; literally, 'a person who is depicted'. This term refers to a representation, especially of the face, of a person.

sôskwâc kâ-isinâkwahk 'realism'; literally, 'just how it looks or appears'. Realism is concerned both with accurate descriptions of the natural world, as it appears to the eye, and with mundane (ordinary, routine) or squalid (depressing) objects or scenes.

kâ-is-âyâk tâpasinahikan 'representational art'. Representational art includes works in which recognizable objects, figures, or elements in nature are depicted, though they may not be entirely realistic in representation. The artist does not necessarily intend to depict an object in the way the eye sees it.

DAY 58

ART TERMS (PART 2)

Here are more of the art terms that Arok Wolvengrey and I originally gathered in 1997. I have spent a lot of time working in galleries, and having exhibitions, and it was natural for me to try and think of the words I could use to describe that piece of my life.

asiniyak kâ-masinipêkâtihcik 'rock paintings'. A rock painting or pictograph is an ancient, stylized painting that has a symbolic meaning. Artist Norval Morrisseau was inspired by rock paintings.

tâpiskôc misiwêyâw 'sculpture'; literally, 'it seems whole'. This is the art of creating forms in three dimensions, either in the round or in relief.

isinâkosiwin 'shape'. A shape is formed whenever a line turns or lines meet, even though an area may not be entirely enclosed. Some examples are: wâwiyêyâw 'circle', isawêyâw 'triangle', and kahkîhkêyâw 'square'.

kâ-mosci-câpasinahikêsihk 'sketch'; literally, 'merely drawing'; a brief account of something through drawing.

ôma kâ-tawâk 'space'; literally, 'here where there is room/space' (a general term for spatial relations).

kâ-isi-tôcikâtêk 'style'; literally, 'how it is done'.

kîkway kâ-nôhtê-tâpasinahamihk 'subject matter'; literally, 'something which [the artist] wishes to depict', for example, objects, people, or ideas.

kiskinowasinâkosiwin 'symbol'. Something that stands for, or suggests, something else by reason of relationship, association, convention, or accidental resemblance.

kâ-âyîtawêyâk 'symmetrical'; literally, 'that which is symmetrical, equal on both sides; that which is two-sided'.

kâ-isi-tôtamihk 'technique'. Refers to the materials used by an artist and the ways these are used in an art work.

kâ-misiwêyâk 'three dimensional'; literally, 'that which is whole'. A form or space occupying depth as well as width and length.

kâ-napakâk 'two dimensional'; literally, 'that which is flat'. A plane or flat surface having length and width but no depth/space.

ita kâ-ohci-kanawâpahtamihk 'viewpoint'; literally, 'from where it is looked at'. The point from which a viewer looks at an object or visual field.

DAY 59

FEELINGS

It is likely that all cultures have terms to express feelings—that is, emotions, notions, sentiments, intuitive sensitivity, and the like. Cree is no different.

môsihtâ 'to feel' (emotions or intuition; or physically).

kaskêyihtamahciho 'to feel lonely, to miss someone'.

miyomahciho 'to feel good'. Note that the stem -(a)mahciho means to feel in terms of health.

mihtâtâw 's/he is grieved, missed'. The verb stem is mihtât-, with a command form: mihtâs. In our traditional culture, people would often cut their hair when mourning. However, I also remember stories of people saying not to cry too much when someone passes away.

pômêh 'to disappoint someone'.

mamîhcih 'to make someone proud'. kimamîhcihin 'you make me proud' = 'I am proud of you'. This works the same as kitatamihin, which means 'you make me smile = (I) thank you'.

pîkwêyihta 'to be worried; to be stressed out'.

pîkiskâtikosi 'to be sad and lonely'.

pakosêyihta 'to be hopeful [of something]': pakosêyimo 'to hope'; the stem -êyiht denotes a mode of thinking (with an inanimate object); -êyim is the animate counterpart (if the thought process involves an animate object).

môcikisi 'to be very happy'.

mistahi nimiywêyihtên 'I am very happy; I like it a lot'.

nitakahkêyihtên 'I am very happy; I think a great deal of it'.

ninôhte-nikamon! 'I want to sing!' (a metaphorical way of saying 'I am happy').

DAY 60

POKER (PART 1)

I remember learning how to play poker when I was eight years old—mind you, this was the old-school form of five-card stud. While gambling is perhaps frowned upon in some polite social circles, as neechies, we have been gambling since the first bannock cooled. We gambled in combat, we gambled when we went out in the winter to hunt, we gambled with hand games, and so on.

Poker in the Texas Hold'em form is simply the most recent form of gambling, and it seems to be something that we are quite good at. Because many Cree people talk about poker, I thought it would be useful to gather some of the words and terminology that describe this part of our lives in contemporary times.

tênikê 'to deal cards'.

otênikês 'dealer'.

kahkiyaw ê-âniskôtapicik 'straight'; literally, 'they are all connected'.

kahkiyaw pîhcâyihk 'all in'.

ê-kakwê-kâsohkwêt 'bluffing'; literally, 'trying to hide his or her face'.

pâmwayês kâ-astêki 'free flop'; literally, 'before they are placed'.

nîswayak nikîsihtân 'full house'; literally, 'I finish it in two ways'.

ascikanak 'chips'; literally, 'something that you wager, put down'.

âstwâhtowin 'gambling'.

nîswascikê/nîsôskân 'to have a pair' or 'a pair'.

otisowaya 'the nuts'; literally, 'his testicles': mitisowayak 'testicles'.

okimâw 'king' (or 'chief').

kihci kâ-yôhtênamihk 'big blind'; literally, 'that which opens things'.

kâ-yôhcênasihk 'little blind'.

sîpiy 'the river'.

DAY 61

HUNTING

My father and all of his uncles went on their last great hunting trip in 1973. I was too young to go along, but I heard about it. It was the last time those old nâpêwak got together and all went hunting as a group. They travelled quickly over their traditional land, and they were in very good shape. While I have always been interested in hunting and the stories of hunting, unfortunately, the only hunting I do is at the grocery store.

One thing many people do not know is that often the Old Women in families were the ones who distributed the meat once it was hunted and prepared. My father told me this about his grandmother, the late Mary Vandall. She was the one who decided how the meat should be given out, and the hunters would respect her wishes in this regard. Unfortunately, I have never seen a story about this written down, but I think that it is important to have this practice noted, to show the importance of women within Cree society.

mâcî 'to hunt [big game]'.

mâcîwin '[big game] hunting'.

omâcîw 'hunter'.

ê-nihtâ-mâcît 's/he is a good hunter'.

ê-mâcîhkâsot 's/he pretends to be a hunter'; a Cree academic; Neal McLeod. cah!

kâsôhikan 'hunting blind'; literally, 'the thing that conceals you'.

pawâkan 'a dream helper'. I have heard many stories of how people would dream of where game was, and would be guided by their pawâkan. Another way to translate the idea of pawâkan might be '[someone's] power source'. They say that one of the daughters of the late James Smith had her power from a frog.

ê-wîhtamâkowisit 'to be told by the powers'; people would often dream about hunting. Although I will never be a hunter, I have seen the ways in which people use the old techniques and apply them to more contemporary times. For instance, my family on Sandy Lake would dream about crops in the same way that they dreamt about hunting. My uncle, the late Burton Vandall, would dream about engines and mechanical problems as well. I suppose we all dream about what we focus on, and we apply some of the old ways to present times.

pâskisikan 'gun'.

aspinahikan 'gun case' (also used as a name for 'condom').

kanâcihtâ pâskisikan 'clean a gun'.

ê-mâtâhât 's/he tracks something'; ê-nâtahâhtât 's/he goes after something by tracking'.

mâcîwaskiy 'hunting territory'.

pâstâhowin 'to have something that you do come back on you, or your loved ones'. This refers to transgressions committed against human beings. You use a different term when someone causes unnecessary suffering to an animal: ohcinêwin.

pimîhkân 'pemmican'; a mixture of berries, meat, and grease (what we went crazy for before KFC).

pisiskiwi-okimâw 'a game warden'; literally, 'a boss of animals'. I heard this word once from Keith Goulet. Couched in this term there is, as is true with many words dealing with government legislation, an element of sarcasm.

DAY 62

ACADEMIC TERMS

The theme for today is academic terms. I thought this might be useful for some graduate students and academics. The trick is to try to translate the metaphor and idea behind the word and not search for a literal translation. It is my firm belief that not only do Cree speakers need to describe the past, but we also need to try to coin words to describe various aspects of contemporary life. I suppose, in many ways, this is the core philosophy of this book.

misi-wanih- 'to make someone lost in a great way' (could be used relative to colonialism). nicâpân used this term, Peter Vandall.

iyinitowiyiniw-kiskêyihtamowin 'Indigenous Knowledge': iyinito- is a stem that means 'everyday, ordinary, common; exemplary' and has connotations of being tied to a specific place and location—or, indeed, context; iyiniw 'person, First Nations person'; kiskêy- ihtamowin 'knowledge'.

tôtamowin 'doing'. A term used by Emma LaRoque to discuss the idea of praxis; of engagement.

osâm mistahi itêyimisowin 'thinking too highly of oneself'. This may be one of the ways of articulating the philosophical foundation that leads to a thinking of binary consciousness between "civilization" and "a state lacking civilization."

wîhtamâkêwin 'telling, announcement, proclamation'; a phrase used in Winona Wheeler's Ph.D. dissertation, "Decolonizing Tribal Histories."

kaskihtamâso 'to earn something for yourself'. My late father used this term a great deal; it could be used to articulate part of the process of gathering information—of Indigenous research protocol, the idea of "putting in the hours."

âcimisowin 'an autobiography'; a story someone tells about himself or herself; the idea of life experience.

kâ-pê-isi-kiskêyihtahk iyinitowiyiniw-kiskêyihtamowin 'the process of coming to know Indigenous Knowledge'. Perhaps we could use this word for 'methodology'. Or possibly: kâ-pê-isi-kiskinwahamâsot 'how one comes to learn [for oneself]'.

tipêyimiso-kiskêyihtamowin 'self-governing knowledge and thinking'. I prefer this translation over 'decolonize' because 'decolonize' implies a reaction to someone external. I think that on some level we need to move beyond this and to generate and retrieve our own knowledge systems.

kiyokê 'visit'; let's use this term instead of the clinical term 'interview'.

kiskinowâpahkê- 'to learn by watching'; engaged; experiential learning. Also consider kiskinowâpahtihiwê- 'teach by showing'.

nêpêwisiwin 'shame, to be ashamed'; the act of being colonized and trying to distance oneself from one's own roots and culture; an internalization of colonial forces (as Fanon would describe it).

môniyâw-wasâsiwin 'settler anxiety'.

âsay kâ-mâmiskôtamihk 'what has already been expounded upon'. Perhaps this could be used as a word for 'literature/source review'.

nîkân-pîkiskwêwina 'introduction'; literally, 'the front words'.

sôniyâw-miyikowin 'grant'; literally, 'money that is given'.

kihci-sôniyâw-miyikowin 'SSHRC (Social Sciences and Humanities Research Council)'; literally, 'the great money that is given'.

manâcihitowin 'respect; where you think of someone highly without regard for yourself'. Perhaps we could use this as a term for 'ethics'.

FOUR CREES RESIST THE BLACKFOOT

FROM *PLAINS CREE TEXTS*

Through the study of our classical vocabulary, we are able to learn the sound pathways of our ancestors, and we are able to construct pathways of sound in the present. Once again, I find these narratives collected by Bloomfield to be particularly rich in this regard. The narrative studied today is interesting because it demonstrates the friendship that mistahi-maskwa and wîhkasko-kisêyin had. It is also interesting because it shows them in combat, and not only in their function as political leaders. All of the old chiefs had demonstrated in their youth their bravery and honour in combat, and this is what gave them the power, at least in part, to later become chiefs.

itê ê-wîkicik nêhiyawak 'where the Crees lived'. This is an interesting and useful expression because the idea of where they lived is not bound to a reserve or a city; the reference is what I would call "spatially open." When I was growing up, perhaps the expression itê ê-wîkicik nêhiyawak would be used in stories bound to a reserve or community. wîki, as a verb, means 'to dwell, to live', whereas 'to live', as in to have life, is pimâtisi (which is cognate with the Anishinaabe bimaadizi).

mâwacihitowak ê-sipwêhtêcik oskinîkiwak 'the young men gathered to depart by foot'. Note that sipwêhtê 'leave, depart' is in the conjunct mode and builds upon the earlier verb. oskinîkiwak means 'young men'. Note that these young men were preparing to go into Blackfoot territory. This gave a sense of purpose and focus. I think this is something young men today crave.

kimoti 'steal'. It is interesting to note that this verb is used to describe 'horse borrowing' from the Blackfoot. It would be interesting to find if the verb nitâhtâmo 'borrow'—nitotamaw- means 'ask for something from someone'—was used in the classical narratives. At any rate, it should be noted that the focus of warfare was not to kill people but rather to demonstrate bravery and honour.

kâ-pimohtêcik 'the ones who are walking'. This term demonstrates that the Crees of old were often in need of horses.

têpakohp tahtwâw ê-nipâcik 'when they had slept seven nights'. Note that the conjunct mode is marked by ê-, which could be translated as 'when'. The nipâ- stem means 'to sleep', têpakohp is 'seven', and tahtwâw is a marker of measurement ('so many times').

kâsôhtawêwak 'they hide from others'. Here the text is referring to the young men who were trying to conceal their positions (kâsô- means 'hide'). Interestingly, in Cree -hkâso means 'to pretend'.

nîso nâpêwak itohtêwak mîkiwâhpihk, misatimwa ê-kimotamawâcik, ê-nipâyit. 'Two men go into a tipi, while the one is sleeping, and they steal a horse'. The elements of this sentence are: nîso 'two'; nâpêwak 'men' (namely the Cree who were part of the raid); itohtê 'to go [by foot]' ("by foot" is implied by the -htê stem—you can make many words with this stem: for example, sâpohtê 'to walk through' and kîskwêhtê 'to walk in a crazy fashion'); mîkiwâhpihk 'in(to), on, at a tipi'; misatimwa 'horses', but the -(w)a ending shows that the horses are obviative participants, less topical in this scenario than some other participants (that is, the Cree, the ones stealing them); kimotamaw- 'steal from someone'; ê-nipâyit 'while they [obviative] were sleeping' (this is in the conjunct mode and also agrees with an obviative participant). Once again the obviative is a third-person form, but it is one step further down from the one doing the main action. So, in a way, the obviative could be considered a form of fourth-person actor. In this case, the obviative referent is not the same as the one in the previous clause. It is the Blackfoot who are sleeping, not the horses.

têhtapiwak, ê-wî-sipwêhtêcik 'they mounted, in order to depart'. Generally, wî- translates as 'will' or 'going to' and denotes a form of intention or conditional possibility (or 'prospective aspect'). Here it functions as a mechanism to create a temporal relation to the first verb and describes the next element after the main verb.

âtawêyim 'to be dissatisfied with someone', 'to reject someone'.

pakwâtêwak ê-mâyatisiyit misatimwa 'they disliked the poor horses'. I think that 'poor' is a better translation, in this context, than the literal 'ugly'. pakwât- is the stem, sometimes translated as 'to hate'.

kiwî-wîcêtinâwâw, oskinîkîtik 'I will go with you, young men'. An Old Man says this to some young men who are involved in the raid. The -itik ending denotes a formal way of addressing people.

mâskôc otinâyêko misatim, ê-itêyimitakok 'I believe that perhaps you will take a horse': mâskôc 'perhaps'; otin 'to take [something animate]' (in contrast to 'steal'); ê-itêyimitakok literally means 'I think this of you (all)', but I think that in this context it might be better translated as 'I think'.

DAY 64

POKER (PART 2)

This is our second look at poker terminology. I think that one of the key ways to build contemporary terminology is by continuing to revisit it and to build on it, by trying to expand on it, and by asking people how they would say words that we may not be sure of. The wonders of the Internet and social media allow us to do this in a way that would never have been possible during the height of the oppression of Indigenous people in Canada, and the repressive measures of the Indian Act, which did not allow us to leave our reserves and communities.

ê-pihêwosicik 'clubs'. Compare this with pihêwosit, pihêwayasit 'prairie chicken foot'.

cîpopêhikanak 'diamonds'.

misipîk 'spades'.

wâyinopêhikana 'hearts'.

kwayask mistakihtêw 'high-stakes poker'; literally, 'it truly costs a great deal'.

sâkaskinêw 'full house'; literally, 'they are packed tightly'. This could also mean that 'the house—dwelling—is full of people'.

nêwopêwak 'four of a kind'.

pêyakopêhikan 'ace'.

yahkina *or* **yahkinasi** 'raise'; literally, 'push it forward (a little)'; perhaps also tahkahcikê—this term is also used for playing pool, billiards.

wêpina 'fold'.

niscos, micâcaht 'three', 'ten' in diminutive form. Note: in cards, the numbers can be given in the diminutive form.

ê-kaskitêsicik 'black flush'.

ê-mihkosicik 'red flush'.

DAY 65

CREE-ENGLISH SLANG

We need slang to keep our language organic and growing, and also to describe the changing world around us. We developed slang in the past, too, and perhaps the strongest example of this was the emergence of Michif. Other Indigenous languages have done this as well.

tâpwê *tight* '[something is] cool, set up, ready to go'.

***cool*wâsin** 'it is cool'.

ê-kî-*realiz*owiyân 'I realized something'.

***porch*ihk** 'at the porch' (the place where the legendary Crow Hop Café was born).

pahkwêsi-*gun* 'a gun that shoots out rays of bannock dough'.

***cha*-wiyinîs** 'the cha man', 'the joker', 'a clown, a goofball'. cah!

***neechi*payiho** 'to become rezified', 'to keep it real', 'to become a neechie', 'to dance with a wolf'. Just don't confuse this with nîhcipayiho- 'to jump down; to throw oneself down'.

***walmart* atâmiskâkêw** 'Walmart greeter'.

wâpiski-*boys*ak 'white boys', 'white friends'.

***walmart*ipicikê** 'to go Walmart shopping'.

***funny*âsin** 'it is funny'.

DAY 66

JOHNNY CASH SONGS

I wish I had a name like Johnny Cash: Neal Sôniyâw! nâh, môy ninahiskên ôma wîhowin 'the name does not really fit me'.

Today, I want to honour one of the patron saints of the Cree Parthenon, Johnny Cash. I used to have *Live at Folsom Prison* on 8-track, and I am not kiyâskisin'. I think I will go on Ebay and try to get this old recording in the old format again. There was nothing like having something tangible like an 8-track in your hand, and seeing the blue light on the machine signalling which program you were on.

nâpêsis, *Sue* kâ-isiyihkâsot 'A Boy Named Sue'.

kipâstâhon 'God's Gonna Cut You Down'.

***Folsom* kipahotowikamikohk** 'Live at Folsom Prison'.

ê-wîsakêyihtamân 'Hurt' (his cover of the classic Nine Inch Nails song).

kâ-kâskitêsîhot 'Man in Black' (and I don't mean a Hutterite—I mean Johnny Cash!).

ispîhk nâpêw takohtêci 'When the Man Comes Around'.

wâsakâm-iskôtêwan 'Ring of Fire'.

kwayask ê-pimohtêyân 'I Walk the Line'.

kêyâpic ê-kaskêyimak awiyak 'I Still Miss Someone'.

nipîkopayin 'Busted'.

25 cipahikanisa kêyâpic '25 Minutes to Go'.

• • •

One of my favourite, and classic, bits of dialogue from *Live at Folsom Prison* is when Johnny asks his roadie, "Bob, mahti minahin nipiy?" ('Bob, can I have some water?'). After Johnny is handed the glass, he then asks, "tâpwê cî ôma nipiy?" ('Is this really water?')—implying that it might be alcohol—êkwa mîna kahkiyaw kâ-kipahikâsocik ê-pâh-pâhpicik ('and with that all of the prisoners laugh').

DAY 67

RODEO

I heard lots of stories from yôtin (the late Charlie Burns). We used to sit around together, and he would talk Cree to me for hours, sometimes. He was like my mosôm, and he guided me along the way through his stories. In fact, about two hundred metres from where I sit writing this, he and my late mosôm cleared a lot of land kayâs long ago.

One of the many stories I remember him telling me was about my câpân, Abel McLeod, who was a rodeo judge here on nihtâwikihcikanisihk (James Smith Reserve). Charlie said, "He really didn't know anything about rodeo, but he was a judge!" I also remember that during these rodeo days on the reserve, the late Edward Ahenakew used to come, and people had a lot of respect for him.

At the suggestion of Sekwun Ahenakew, I began to search for words relating to rodeo. Sometimes words take a while to find, and sometimes, as we search for words, we are surrounded by fields of other stories and sound.

kwêtâsiskâsiwêw-otâpânâsk 'chuckwagon'.

okotiskâwê-otâpânâsk 'chuckwagon'; literally, 'racing wagon'.

tâpakwê-wêpinikêwin 'steer roping'. The stem tâpakwê means to 'snare' and wêpinikêwin means 'throwing'. Compounded then, this literally means 'to snare by throwing a rope' (the "steer" part of the word is implied).

mostoso-nakwâcikêwak 'they are steer roping'.

ê-têhtapi-kîsikâk 'rodeo'; literally, 'the day of riding, of sitting on top of'.

iyâpêwa ê-têhtapit 'bull riding'.

mâyatihk-têhtapiwin 'mutton busting'. As noted in Day 11, in some regions, mâyatihkwayâniyiniwak 'sheepskin people' was used for Russians.

mahkahk 'barrel'.

môhkwâkanêwikamikohk ê-wiyasiwêt 'rodeo judge'; literally, 'the one who judges from the building where horses buck'.

môhkwâkanêwatim 'bucking bronco'. Another word for this is cahkosôkanatim.

môhcowiyiniw 'clown'.

DAY 68

FINGERS AND HANDS

Hands play a key role in our communication, and I know through my work as a visual artist that they are amongst the most interesting and challenging things to draw.

micihciy 'hand' (from the stem form -cihciy). One of my câpâns had a name derived from this. Her name was cîhcam, meaning, to the best of my knowledge, 'hand that is close to me'. When she was older, younger grandchildren used to guide her around, and she in turn would call them nicihciy 'my hand'. Thus, as far as I can tell, cîhcam is a reflected version of this, with the -(i)m ending marking it as something personal and close to you.

yiyîkicihcân 'finger'.

wâstinikê 'to wave'. This word also has connotations of 'hitchhiking' as it describes the action of 'flagging down a ride'.

itwahikanicihcân 'index finger'; literally, 'the finger that you point with': itwahikê- 'to point'.

âhcanicihcân 'ring finger'. This is, no doubt, a fairly recent name for this finger due to the introduction of Christianity and the practice of wearing a ring. It would be interesting to find the older word for this finger.

wanaskocihcân 'fingertip'. This combines wanasko- (wanaskoc 'at the end, at the tip') with the stem for finger, -cihcân.

sôpahcikê 'eat finger-licking good food'. Maybe a slang word for Cree people could be osôpahcikêwak.

maskasiy 'fingernail' (from the stem -askasiy). Note that the stem for 'claw' is the same.

pakamicihcêhamâ 'to clap'. The two stems are pakam- 'to hit, bang', and -cihc- 'finger/hand'—so literally this means 'to bang or hit hands together'. Note that there seems to be an alternating between using -cîhcân and -cihciy as compounding stems for 'fingers'. Arok Wolvengrey tells me this is -cihciy and a shorter form -cihc-, which combines with verbal -ê (for example, cimicihcê- 'to have short hands'), which changes to –â when nominalized by -n (for example, cimicihcân 'a short hand').

isiniskê 'to make hand signals'; the classic form of Indian communication; the neechie lingua franca.

• • •

I once heard a very interesting story from my late father's old friend, Pat Cayan, who was a paratrooper in the legendary 101st Airborne Division. Pat heard this story from the late John Tootoosis. John had told Pat that one time a Crow Indian was in the Battlefords area. He met a Cree along the river at some point. They could not understand each other's spoken language so they used "sign language" to communicate with each other. That system of communication was so good that they could make each other laugh, which shows that the old language would have had the capacity for metaphor and double meaning. The sky was open and clear, and their day was full of stories.

DAY 69

TRANSPORTATION

Since there have been nêhiyawak in the world, we have always found various ways of getting from one place to the next. Be it by astral travel, horses, cars, or now mini-vans, neechies have always found a way to get to a meeting, a battle, to see loved ones, or to see if the bingo balls will bounce their way. The list below includes not only traditional ways of transportation but also contemporary ones.

sêhkêpayîs 'car'; literally, 'the little thing that moves itself'. The stem sêhkê- seems to denote a reflexive action: 'to power oneself' or maybe even 'automatic'? I have never heard this stem compounded anywhere else—of course that could be because of the limitations of my Cree.

otâpânâsk 'truck' or 'wagon'; literally, 'the wooden thing that transports things'.

kinoyaw-otâpânâsk 'bus'; literally, 'long-bodied vehicle'.

pimâciho 'to travel'; 'to make a living'.

naskwên 'to pick someone up'.

pôsi 'to get into a vehicle'. I have also used it to mean to 'get on a ride at the fair' (which seems fair enough).

sipwêkocin 's/he leaves by a mechanical vehicle [by water, land, or air]'.

sipwêcimê 'leave by a canoe'.

takokocin 's/he arrives by a moving vehicle'.

twêhômakan 'it lands' (inanimate—for example, a plane). The stem for a living creature to land would be twêho-. The ending -makan indicates that the plane is inanimate.

DAY 70

ILLNESSES

We Cree have always had our medicines and ceremonies and, of course, our relatives to help us get through physical illnesses and in our times of greatest need.

We should never forget that our Old People were gifted with various plants and medicines that allowed them to heal not only their bodies but also the deeper core of their beings. My one grandmother, cîhcam, who was the niece of atâhk-akohp, used her hands to help people heal, in the same manner that people use reiki today.

mâyimahciho 'to feel badly', which is one of the first stages of an illness: mâyi- 'bad, ugly'; -mahciho 'to feel [in such a way]'.

mâyimahcihowin 'influenza'. Although this can also mean simply 'ill health' or 'feeling bad', it can also specifically refer to influenza. One of my grandmothers had a medicine made from skunk bladder that helped people survive influenza.

sôkâwâspinêwin 'diabetes'; literally, the 'sugar sickness'. sôkâw is borrowed from English 'sugar' or French 'sucre'; -âspinêwin is 'disease; illness'. An alternative term is sîwinikanâspinêwin: sîwinikan 'sugar; sweetener'.

macâspinêwin 'sexually transmitted disease'; literally, 'the bad ailment'.

kihci-macâspinêwin 'the exceptionally bad ailment; HIV'.

misi-omikîwin 'smallpox'; literally, 'the big scabbiness'. I don't think we can underestimate the effect that this disease must have had on the Cree people (and other Indigenous peoples).

nipahomikîw 's/he dies of smallpox'.

manicôsak 'cancer'; literally, 'little bugs'.

ostostota 'cough'.

câhcâmo 'sneeze'.

DAY 71

BEING CREE
FROM *WÂSKAHIKANIWIYINIW-ÂCIMOWINA* *(STORIES OF THE HOUSE PEOPLE)*

Today's words and phrases are from Peter Vandall's (kôkôcîs) narration "Being Cree" from the book *wâskahikaniwiyiniw-âcimowina* (*Stories of the House People*), which was edited and translated by the late Freda Ahenakew.

This book was the first of the many books Freda published to help give us a strong anchor for our language in contemporary times. She, along with my late nôhkom, Ida McLeod, played a key role in standardizing Cree orthography, making it much easier for us to dwell in the written texts of Cree. We owe both of these women a great deal, as they set the foundation for our use of written Cree in contemporary times.

nêhiyâsisak 'the young Crees'; nicâpân is talking about young people today and how they seemingly try to distance themselves from Cree.

tâpiskôc 'like, it seems'. There is more to this meaning, though. nicâpân uses this expression (and the slight variation, tâpiskôt) repeatedly to articulate the idea 'it seems as though, it appears'. Thus, when using this word while talking about the behaviour of young people, the behaviour gains an indefinite quality. This little expression tâpiskôc gives some space for things to change, opens up the possibility for young people to alter their behaviour.

môniyâw-kiskêyihtamowin 'white man's knowledge', which seemingly, at times, contradicts nêhiyaw-kiskêyihtamowin 'Cree knowledge'.

osk-âyak 'young beings; young ones': oski- 'young'; ay- 'one; being' (-ak pluralizes it). oski-ayak is normally contracted in speech to osk-âyak.

mistahi ê-nêpêwihikocik 'they are very ashamed; it makes them ashamed' (note that this is prefaced by tâpiskôc): mistahi 'a lot; a great deal' (for example, mistahi-maskwa 'Big Bear' means a 'whole lot of bear'); nêpêwih- 'to make someone feel shy or ashamed'.

namôya ê-nisitohtamohkâsocik 'they pretend to not understand': namôya 'no, not' (often shortened to môy—in the 1800s it was written as nama wiya); nisitohta 'to understand'; -hkâso 'to pretend'.

tâpiskôt namôya kîkway ê-itêyihtahkik onêhiyâwiwiniwâw 'it is as though they think nothing of their Creeness': namôya kîkway is, literally, 'no thing', 'no entity' (often also simply nama kîkway, which is in and of itself linguistic evidence for an earlier form of nama wiya); itêyihta- 'to think thus; to conceptualize something so'; onêhiyâwiwiniwâw 'their Creeness'. My translation varies slightly from the late Freda Ahenakew's, which was 'it is as if their Creeness means nothing to them'. Once again, nicâpân uses the word tâpiskôt, which gives the people he is speaking about some latitude to change their actions.

pêyakwâw 'once [upon a time]'; the past may be implied here but the word refers to a specific time and so differs from the more generic reference to past time of kayâs 'long ago'.

ê-kî-tipêyihtahkik 'they owned [it]', referring to the territory that Cree-speaking people owned; Indigenous people had clear concepts of territory and space.

ispîhcâ- 'extend so far; be so big; be of such a quantity' (referring to the land of this country).

kikiska 'wear [something] like clothing'; 'to have [something] be part of your being'. In the context of this story, the word is used to talk about nêhiyâwiwin 'Creeness'; the late Freda Ahenakew translates this as 'it is part of them'; my late father used the same stem to describe the effects of residential schools: ê-kikiskâkoyahk 'we wear it', 'we wear the effects of the experience of the school process'. Interestingly, my father appears to have used the inverse form (kikiskaw- *plus* -iko), possibly suggesting a more active role of the experience in our lives.

DAY 72

SOCIAL CONTROL (PART I)

FROM *WÂSKAHIKANIWIYINIW-ÂCIMOWINA* *(STORIES OF THE HOUSE PEOPLE)*

Today we examine terms from another of Peter Vandall's narratives, as recounted in *wâskahikaniwiyiniw-âcimowina* (*Stories of the House People*). Within this narrative, there is a discussion of Cree law and how people related to each other in previous times. This points to the strength of Cree-speaking people, demonstrating the way in which they related to, and regulated interactions with, one another. More of these types of narratives should be examined so that we can revive our classical legal concepts and then try to apply these "principles of law" to contemporary times.

ê-kî-is-ôhpikinâwasot 'how they raised their children'. In the context of the narrative, it refers to how Cree people raised their children. The flavouring particle isi- literally means 'manner in which something occurs'. The most common Cree word that most people know, tânisi, is a compound of this stem and tân-, which is a multipurpose element like the "wh" that begins English question words. ohpikinâwaso means 'to raise children'.

kî-mihcêtiw nêhiyaw 'there were many Crees': mihcêtiwak 'there are many'. This is interesting, since the singular is used but Crees as a collective are implied. Another way of saying 'there are lots [of something]' is to add -skâ to the end of a noun. For example, sakimês means 'mosquito', but sakimêskâw means 'there are lots of mosquitoes'.

akâmôtênaw 'across the camp circle'. akâm- means 'across'. The other stem in the compound is ôtênaw, which today means 'town'. Thus, the etymological stem of the word denotes a collective living space. The idea that urbanization is a recent phenomenon (since the 1960s) may be a somewhat misguided concept.

akâmaskiy 'overseas' is often used for Europe, but can also mean "overseas" in a more generic sense. I remember, years ago, a young man from Korea came to my late father's when we were going to have a sweat. The young man wanted an "Indian name." So my father jokingly said, "ahâw, akâmaskîwiyinîs."

ê-kî-misi-wîhkwêstêki mâna mîkiwâhpa 'so big was the circle of these tipis': misi 'large, big'; wîhkwêstê- 'to be situated in a circle'; mîkiwâhp 'tipi'.

wîhkât 'rare; seldom; never' (when used in conjunction with a negative particle like namôya), referring to the lack of crime against each other. It would be helpful to trace the narrative origins of these comments. Perhaps we could draw upon these ideas today.

k-êsi-mâyinikêhkâtocik 'to do bad things to each other'; ka-isi-contracts to k-êsi-; mâyinikê 'to do bad things' can be broken down to the root mây(i)- 'bad, evil' *plus* -(i)n, which means 'action by hand' *plus* the general object marker -ikê. To this is added -ihkaw and –ito, contracted to -hkâto, to create reciprocal action.

nanâtohkêskân 'different nations'. During the pre-reserve period it was common for Assiniboine (Nakota) and Saulteaux to become integrated in Cree camps through kinship.

ê-kî-miyo-wîcêhtocik 'they lived well together': kî- indicates past tense; miyo- 'good, nice, beautiful'; wîcê(h) 'to accompany'; -to indicates, again, the reciprocal.

ê-kanawêyihtahkik êwako ôma 'they took care of this'. The late Freda Ahenakew translates this as 'the people who were responsible for this', but the phrase's etymological roots are 'caring for something'; 'watching over something' (referring to those who were safeguarding institutions).

simâkanisak 'police'.

nâpêhkâso 'to be inducted into the okihcitâwak' (*see* Day 4). I always puzzled over this because of the compounding of the two stems. The two pieces literally are nâpê- 'male; to be a man' and -hkâso 'to pretend', and so 'pretend to be a man; simulate a man'. I have never understood why this would describe joining these societies, except that in the proper context, this stem also means 'be brave'.

pîhtêyâsk 'at the centre pole'. This particle includes pîht(ê)- 'in; inside; inner' and -âsk(w) 'wood, tree'.

ê-wiyasiwâtahkik 'they make rulings; they make decisions'.

pimipici 'to move camp'. pim(i)- 'along; in succession'; pici- 'to move camp'.

DAY 73

SOCIAL CONTROL (PART 2)
FROM *WÂSKAHIKANIWIYINIW-ÂCIMOWINA* (*STORIES OF THE HOUSE PEOPLE*)

Here is the second part of my annotation of nicâpân's narrative "Social Control" (*see* Day 72). The text is an interesting commentary on Cree social institutions. There is much to learn from these types of narratives, and I try to think of how we can apply their lessons to today's world. This is indeed the challenge. But when we weave the classical narratives into a contemporary context, we see that Indigenous consciousness is very powerful, organic, and dynamic. It also demonstrates the resiliancy of nêhiyawak and the persistance of Cree narrative memory.

kîsasiwâtam 's/he makes rulings; s/he makes plans for the community'. Perhaps one could translate this as 'making public policy'.

ê-wâsakâhtêcik 'they walk around [the camp]': wâsakâ- 'around; in a circular fashion'; -htê is a verb-final element that denotes 'walking'.

kahkiyaw ayisiyiniwa 'all people'. In this case, ayisiyiniw ends in an obviative -a, rather than the regular plural -ak, presumably because some other third-person participant is more topical in the current context.

ôtênaw ê-ispîhcâk 'as far as the stretch of the camp'. In the previous narrative, nicâpân used ê-ispîhcâk to include 'the stretch of Canada'. Perhaps, mâmitonêyihcikan ê-ispîhcâk could be translated as 'the stretch of thinking'; or, another poetic rendering, kâ-pawâtamihk ê-ispîhcâk could be translated as 'the stretch of dreaming'.

kî-pimitisahamwak 'they followed it'.

kîkisêpâ 'early in the morning'. kîkisêpâ-mîcisowin means 'breakfast'; wâpâsi means 'to get up early'.

nikî-pêhtawâwak mâna kêhtê-ayak 'I used to hear the Old Ones': pêhtaw (VTA) 'to hear someone'; mâna is a flavouring particle meaning 'usually, always'. The teaching of the Old Ones is the foundation of Cree social institutions.

piyêsîsak kâ-kitocik 'birds sang'. The stem kito- means 'for an animal to make a sound'—although I have only heard it in the context of birds. It is used for Thunderbirds as well; and the expression ê-kitocik can mean 'they are calling out' or 'there is thunder'.

mistahi kâ-takahkihtâkosicik 'those who truly sound beautiful'.

ê-naskwahamawâcik 'they answered someone in sound'.

ê-kî-miywâsiniyik ita ê-kî-pimâcihocik 'their journey through life was very beautiful'.

ihtako- 'to be; to exist; to be there'.

kakêskihkêmo- The late Freda Ahenakew translated this stem as 'to preach', but I think 'to counsel' would be a more appropriate translation. I think that the counselling process, kakêskihkêmowin, is the foundation of classical Cree institutions.

mâyinikê- 'to do something bad'.

mâyi-tôtâto- 'to harm one another'.

tâpiskôc ôki ayamihêwiyiniwak '[they are] like the clergy'. This was uttered in a positive context. The narrator was a member of the Sandy Lake Reserve, where Cree Anglican priests, such as the late Edward Ahenakew, played a key role. In addition to being a clergy member, he was also very active in the League of Indians.

ê-kî-itâpatisicik 'that was their purpose' (referring to the function of counselling).

SEEING AND SIGHT

Sight is one of the most important senses, and the Cree language is loaded with visual imagery and the attempt to render this imagery into words. The words below show the variety of stems: some of them begin with wâp- for 'vision, sight' and require appropriate endings, while others have preceding and following elements added to -(w)âp-, meaning 'sight, eyesight; eyes'. Such a variation in stem types, to me, shows the dynamic nature of the Cree language.

wâpahta 'look at something; see it'.

wâpam 'look [at someone]; see him/her'.

itâpisin 'to have such a view [of something]'.

miskîsik 'eye'. Louise Halfe once suggested that this was perhaps a collapsed form of misi-kîsik, which would mean 'the big heavens/ sky'. This a very poetic way of describing eyes: "big heavens" that hold visual reality.

mahkacâpiw 's/he has big eyes'; -âpi (or wâpi- or -acâpi) is a common stem to denote 'sight' or 'eyes'. ê-mâh-mahkacâpipayit means 'his or her eyes suddenly got big' (-payi is 'to become' and also denotes sudden movement; mâh- denotes reduplication, repeated action).

itâpahkân 'a spyglass'.

kîmôtâpi 'to sneak a glance'. (If an attractive person is walking by, and you want to sneak a peek, and then tell a story about it—this is the word for you.)

sôhkê-wâpam 'to stare at someone'; literally, 'to look at someone strongly'.

apisicâpisi 'to have small eyes'.

sîpihkocâpi 'to have blue eyes'.

minôsâpi 'to have cat eyes'.

pâskâpi 'to be blind'; literally, 'have an eyeball that burst' (by accident or injury, and therefore be blind). One can also say namôya wâpiw 's/he is blind; s/he does not see'.

-nâkwan 'to appear [as something]; to appear [in such a way]'. Combined with an initial element, this describes the appearance of something inanimate.

-nâkosi- 'for a person to appear [as something]; to look [like something]'. Combined with an initial element, this will describe the appearance of something animate.

DAY 75

INCREASE, MOVE FORWARD, EXPAND

I am a bit of a neechie nerd. For fun, sometimes I read and study the dictionary that nitôtêm, Arok Wolvengrey, put together. It has occurred to me that it would be an interesting exercise to go through Arok's dictionary and build lists of words around particular stems. I think this would be a way to start to cross-reference various words and, indeed, would be a first step toward creating a thesaurus in Cree. The list below is an initial attempt at this, built from words that can wrap around the stem yahki-.

yahki- 'the act of pushing forward; to increase; to grow; to expand'.

yahkaham 's/he pushes it forward'. Note: the additional stem ending -ah implies the action of the verb is occurring through a tool.

yahkakocin 'to increase in speed'; ya-yahkakocin is 'to increase in speed greatly'.

yahkakihtam 's/he raises the price of something'.

yahkakihtamowin 'inflation'.

yayahkakihtamopayiwin 'rapid inflation'.

yahki-nôtinikês 'the vanguard in a military unit'. I coined this word, using the yahki- stem.

yahkinam 's/he pushes something'; the -(i)n verb-final element ending implies that the action of the verb is being realized through the use of the hand.

yahkisîhtâw 's/he makes something larger'; (o)sîhtâw- is compounded with the stem yahki-.

yahkisîhtâwimo I coined this word to mean 'he makes something bigger through words, through talking'. In this compound I used the word yahkisîhtâw (see previous entry) and the -mo ending for 'sound', 'speech', or 'words'.

yahkîmowin 'increase of family; increase of population'.

yahkohtêw 's/he goes forward'; literally, 's/he moves forward by walking'.

yahkipahtâw 's/he goes forward by running'.

yahki-âniskopita 's/he pushes it further by connecting'.

yâhkasin 'it is light in weight'; (wordplay: as this stem is similar but the 'a' is long). Perhaps yahki-yâhkasin 'it increases in being light [weight]' could be used for describing space travel and gravity.

yahkisina 'push wood farther into the fire'.

DAY 76

LEONARD COHEN SONGS

Some of my fondest memories growing up with my late father are of the endless days we spent hunting moose, tracking game quietly all day, and sitting patiently in the hunting blinds. Kidding—I don't know how to hunt. But I do remember listening to Leonard Cohen with my father many times, and today whenever I hear Cohen's throaty rasp, I always think of my late father.

As the Cree language continues to grow and develop, I think it is important for us to translate the English world around us into Cree. The layering and merging of these languages is an important part of the process for keeping Cree alive, as it helps us to anchor the language in our contemporary experiences. Here are some of Leonard Cohen's song (and album) titles translated into Cree.

nikamowina mêskanâhk ohci 'Songs from the Road' (mêskanaw-nikamowina would work as well).

kinâpêm niya 'I'm Your Man'.

ôtê nîkânihk 'The Future'.

kâ-kisêwâtiskwêwak 'Sisters of Mercy'.

kâ-nanakîstam 'The Partisan'; literally, 'the one who resists'; I thought that this was a better way of translating what a partisan is, rather than calling him or her a rebel.

piyêsîs pîwâpiskwêyâpîhk 'Bird on the Wire'.

Chelsea kâpêsiwikamik 'Chelsea Hotel'.

piponiskwêw 'Woman of Winter'.

sôsân 'Suzanne'.

kîhtwâm mêriyân 'So Long, Marianne' (or êkosi mâka, mêriyân).

awîna awa ôta cîkiskôtêhk 'Who by Fire'.

otina ôma akâwâtamowin 'Take this Longing'.

kihci-sîpihko-kimiwanasâkay 'Famous Blue Raincoat'.

nîmihin isko sâkihitowin pônipayiki 'Dance Me to the End of Love'.

hoka hey! 'Hallelujah' (or ânênôya).

pê-ati-tipiskâw 'Night Comes On'.

kâ-isi-pôni-nôcihiskwêwêt 'Death of a Ladies' Man'.

DAY 77

OFFICE

I work in an office—as a professor at a university—and the words of the office are the words of my everyday life. I compiled the list of words below so I could most accurately describe this part of my world, which I think is a part of the world of many people who draw upon the Cree language.

masinahikan-sâkipicikan 'file drawer'; literally, 'something you pull out that is related to books'.

masinahikanapiwin 'desk'; literally, 'the thing associated with books where you sit'.

tahkikamâpôhkâkan 'water cooler'.

okimâsis 'boss'; literally, 'the little chief'. This is also a family name from White Bear First Nation and at Beardy's and Okemasis (okimâsis) First Nation.

pîkiskwêmocikanis 'cell phone'. Other words that are in use are diminutives for 'phone' include: sêwêpicikanis 'little ringer' and ayimâkanis 'little talking thing'.

osâm ê-atoskêt 'burnout'; literally, 's/he works too much'.

mâmawapiwin 'meeting'.

mâmawapiwikamikos 'meeting room'.

mînwasinahikanâpoy 'Liquid Paper'.

akohkwahikan 'stapler'. This is related to the term for welding discussed in Day 39's list.

masinatahikê 'to type'.

masinatahikan 'typewriter' or 'keyboard'.

âpakosîs 'mouse'.

DAY 78

INTERACTING WITH OUR CHILDREN (PART 3)

It is my firm belief that the future of the Cree language rests in our children (kitawâsimisinawak). If we take the time to talk to them, and teach them all of the Cree that we know, we can create vessels for our language that will transfer Cree to coming generations. Children, like I remember my late father saying, are on loan to us from the Creator—we owe it to them to provide all of the threads and fabrics of our language so they can clothe themselves with ancestral memory.

kîkwây ê-kî-kiskinohamâkosiyan anohc kiskinohamâtowika-mikohk? 'What did you learn at school today?': kîkwây 'what'; kiskinohamâkosi- 'to learn'; anohc 'today'; kiskinohamâtowikamik 'school'; and the locative -ohk, which you could translate as 'at [school]'.

atamiskaw 'shake his or her hand; greet him/her'.

manâcim kikâwiy 'respect your mother'.

kimamihcihin 'you make me proud' (maybe you could say this if your child did well on a test).

kinaspitawâw kimosômipan 'you resemble your late grandfather'. I remember nicâpân (my great-grandfather) used to say that I resembled his grandfather, and that has always meant a lot to me.

sakiniskênin *or* **sakicihcênin** 'hold my hand'. Both -cihc- and -nisk- can refer to the hand (for example, micihciy 'hand'), but -nisk- is generally only found in verbs and some particles (for example, kihciniskêhk 'on the right-hand side').

tânisi ê-itêyihtaman ôma? 'What do you think of this?'. My late father used to say this to me a lot when I was a kid. He did this not only to show that he valued my opinions but also because he wanted to teach me independence.

mêtawâkan 'toy'.

wahwâ! 'Oh, my goodness!'. Anyone who has children knows that this is a phrase that can be used in a variety of situations.

mahti miyin anima 'please pass me that'.

kimiyohtwân 'you are kind, you are good-natured'.

mahti minah kôhkom maskihkîwâpoy 'get your kôhkom some tea'. minah- is the VTA stem for 'getting someone a liquid/drink'.

FALL

The fall has always been my favourite season—the start of the school year, the change in the colour of the leaves, and the crispness of the air. I remember the combines and their lights, moving around on the crops at night. I always remember the Americans who would come and work together and who could quickly harvest a field. They were called custom combiners.

takwâkin 'fall [season], autumn'; takwâkiki 'in the fall; when it will be fall'. I believe that it refers to the leaves that fall on the ground.

ê-mâh-masinipêpayiki nîpiya 'the leaves change to many colours'. I have tried for many years to find a phrase in English that translates this elegantly—as elegantly as Cree is able to express this, and many other things—rather than in the clumsy way that I am proposing.

kâspihtâkwan 'it sounds of crispness' (that is, the crunching of leaves).

takwâki-pîsim 'fall moon'.

mikiskon 'to be late fall; early freeze-up'.

pawahikê 'to thresh, to combine' (a farming term: *see* Day 39). I remember while growing up I was always intrigued by combining. Some very persistent farmers would combine late into the night, until the wheat got "tough" (or wet). I always thought that there was something poetic about the lights of combines in the vastness of a dark night. The night, like a great dark ocean.

âhcipici- 'to move'. I associate the fall with moving. Maybe I moved to start a new program, a new school—it always seemed to me like fall was a time for change. My late father, nôhtâwîpan, helped me move many times with his old Ford truck.

osâwisîho 'to be dressed in orange'. This could be the orange of hunting outfits that move through the forest.

sîpêkiskâwasâkay 'sweater'; sîpêkiskâw- refers to the stretchiness of the material used in this particular type of -asâkay 'garment; dress, jacket, coat, etc.'. As the fall season progresses, it certainly begins to get colder. In Michif, the word for sweater is chemish, from French chemise.

piyêsîsak ê-ati-pimihâcik sâwanohk isi 'the birds begin to fly south'.

ati-tahkipêpayin 'the water begins to cool'.

kîhtwâm ê-kiskinohamâkosicik 'they are learning again' (that is, back to school).

DAY 80

BUFFALO

The buffalo plays a key role in Cree culture, narrative history, and language. All across the Great Plains, the nêhiyawak (Cree) relied heavily upon the animals for their livelihoods. Many of my ancestors from the wâskahikaniyiniwak (the House People), as well as my relatives and ancestors from the nihtâwikihcikanisihk area (James Smith First Nation), would have hunted buffalo. As such, one cannot underestimate the effect that the loss of the great herds would have had upon the Crees. Where I teach at Trent University there are a lot of students of Irish ancestry. I often suggest that the loss of the buffalo would have been similar (with differences) to the potato famine for the Irish.

It is interesting to note that many Old Cree People believed that part of their physical strength was derived from the buffalo. They thought that because the animal was free and roamed around, it was a strong animal. At first, many Old Cree and Blackfoot thought that cattle were not as smart and strong as buffalo, and so they were reluctant to eat them. So highly valued were buffalo that many interesting metaphors and other terms that drew upon them developed in our language—we will explore a few of these below.

paskwâw-mostos 'buffalo'.

paskwâw-mostos-awâsis 'Buffalo Child'; the key figure in the classic Cree narrative that expounds upon teachings of wâhkôhtowin 'kinship' centred upon the mistasiniy 'grandfather stone'.

mistasiniy 'grandfather stone'; literally, 'the big stone', and understood as the 'Grandfather Buffalo stone').

nikwêmês kisêyinîs 'my namesake Old Man' (referring to Old Man Buffalo).

môsâpêw 'bachelor'. This word is used to describe the males that would be on the side of a herd. Historically, it is unclear which usage came first and was metaphorically extended to the other.

paskwâw-mostoswayân 'buffalo hide'. I remember that my late father once pulled out a buffalo hide and told me that if I ever got sick, I was to wrap a buffalo hide around me, and that it would help me get better. It reminds me of the story of Joseph Beuys (an influential twentieth-century artist) in World War II when, as a German fighter pilot, he was shot down and nursed back to health by people in Crimea. He did an installation piece years later in which he remembered the warm hides that were placed around him.

pimîhkân 'pemmican'. Made with grease, berries, and buffalo meat, pimîhkân was a food staple during the fur trade. I think the important role of pimîhkân during the fur trade demonstrates the strength and positionality of Indigenous women at the time.

pîhtokahânapiwiyin 'Poundmaker', the well-known Cree–Assiniboine leader; his father was sikâkwayân 'Skunk-hide'. Poundmaker's name can be broken into the following elements: pîhtokahân 'buffalo pound' (which can also be said and written as pîhtikwahân); api 'to sit'; and -iyin 'man' (a shortened form of iyiniw).

paskwâw-mostos otisiy 'buffalo belly-button; the crocus', a purple flower that blooms in May.

mihkominisa 'buffalo berries'. This is also the name of a lake that played such an important part in my ancestors' lives, mihkomin-sâkahikan (Redberry Lake). A literal 'buffalo berries' would likely be mostosomina.

mostoswaskasiy 'buffalo hoof'.

mostosonâhk 'buffalo country'.

mostos sometimes 'buffalo' is simplified to this stem, but this stem by itself also means 'cow'.

paskwâw-mostososoy 'buffalo tail'.

paskwâw-mostosostikwânikan 'buffalo skull'. My friend Joseph Naytowhow tells a funny story about kistêsinaw putting a paskwâw-mostosostikwânikan on his own head.

paskwâw-mostoso-wîhkask 'buffalo sage'.

paskwâw-moscosos *or* **paskwâw-moscosis** 'buffalo calf'.

omikikwayaw 'scabby neck'—the original name of Fineday. The context here is important. Wes Fineday told me this story once. When he was a young man, his câpân (Fineday) was named 'scabby neck', a metaphor referring to buffalo fighting. Bull buffalo would get scabby necks after their fighting and combat with one another. This is an example where context is everything.

DAY 81

PREVERBS

The backbone of Cree grammar is compounding—bringing verb stems and preverbs together. In fact, I have witnessed many "compounding duels," where Crees try to outdo each other to see who can make the most outrageous and complex compounded words. Our language is a natural one for poetry and rich description. My dream is for us to start writing whole books solely in Cree (with a parallel English translation like the late Freda Ahenakew's books). The particles below occur before a verb; they function, in a sense, like adverbs.

ati- 'becoming; progressing toward'. Some examples: ati-kimiwan 'it starts to rain'; ê-ati-nêhiyawêt 's/he starts to speak Cree'.

nôhtê- 'want'. Some examples: ê-nôhtê-sipwêhtêyan cî? 'Do you want to leave?'; ê-nôhtê-kapêsiyan cî ôta? 'Do you want to camp here?'.

mosci- this preverb implies that something is merely done without augmentation, or in the simplest form or most normal form. Some examples: ê-mosci-wîc-âyâmitocik 'they just live together' (in the sense of 'they are not married'); mosci-nêhiyawêw 's/he speaks straight Cree' (no English mixed in).

miyo- 'well; beautiful; good'. Some examples: ê-miyo-nikamot 's/he sings well'; ê-miyonâkosit 's/he looks beautiful'.

kakwê- 'try'. Some examples: ê-kakwê-atoskêt nêtê 's/he tries to work over there'; ê-kakwê-pîkiskwâtak 'I try to talk to her/him'.

nitawi- (nitô-) 'to go; to go off and do something'. Some examples: ê-kî-nitaw-âtoskêt 's/he went off to work'; ê-kî-nitawi-nôtinikêt 's/he went off to fight' (for example, to war).

nihtâ- 'to do something well; be skilled at something'. Some examples: ê-nihtâ-nêhiyawêt 's/he speaks Cree well'; ê-nihtâ-kaskikwâsot 's/he is good at sewing'.

sôhki- *or* **/sôhkê-/** 'hard, strongly, forcefully'. Some examples: ê-sôhkê-atoskêt 's/he works hard'; ê-sôhkê-mêtawêt 's/he plays hard'.

kwayasko- 'straight, properly, correctly'. Some examples: ê-kwayasko-nahascikêt 's/he cleans up properly'; ê-kwayask-itôtahk anima 's/he does that properly'. It is also possible to use kwayask independently: kwayask ê-nahascikêt 's/he cleans up properly'; kwayask ê-itôtahk anima 's/he does that properly'.

acici- 'upside down, head downward'. Some examples: acicipayin 'it moves downwards' (could be used for the stock market); ê-acici-pimihâmakahk 'it flies upside down' (for example, a plane).

DAY 82

PRACTICAL VERBS

As a follow-up to the previous discussion about preverbs, I thought that it would be good to examine some practical verbs. These are verbs that help describe everyday life. One verb can do a lot to describe the world around you, and learning basic verbs can help you to move to a point where you can describe the whole world around you in Cree. One useful exercise that I have found is to make a list of words that I want to learn each day and then look them up in a Cree dictionary. Over time, this helps you develop your vocabulary in a contextualized fashion.

I encourage everyone to learn. I was fortunate to hear Cree all my life, but it wasn't until I was in my early twenties that I really started to stitch sentences together. Whatever work you do to learn Cree and to foster Cree will be the legacy that you leave for your children.

âstam 'come here'. This is really a particle that functions like an interjection and can't be used like other verbs.

atoskê 'work'.

pamihcikê 'drive a vehicle; manage things'. nicâpân, kôkôcîs, used to say ê-pamihak sêhkêpayîs 'I manage a car'. This is pakaskinêhiyawêwin, kayâs-school Cree.

pâhpi 'laugh'. You know you are Cree if you like to laugh. They may take our country, but they cannot take our jokes and laughter (holeh—I sound like Braveheart here).

pasikô 'stand up'.

nakî 'stop'; nakîpayi 'to park a car'.

wâsaskotênikê 'turn the lights on'.

âstawêpita 'turn the lights out'. âstawêha is the stem for 'putting out a fire' or 'a fire going out'. This is an example of Crees using an old metaphor to explain new things.

kocihtâ 'try something'.

âpacihtâ 'use something'.

sipwêhtê 'leave' (implies motion by walking).

pimipahtâ 'run'.

itohtê 'go' (can but does not necessarily refer to motion by walking).

mâcihtâ 'start something'.

pîhtwâ 'smoke'; mahti pîhtwâhin 'please give me a smoke'.

DAY 83

LITERARY THEORY

Being a neechie nerd, I love to try to find ways of using Cree to translate interesting ideas from my academic study. Some of these may be way out there, but I hope you find value in some of them. The theme today is literary theory—my basic philosophy is that the heart of Indigenous Knowledge exists in our stories and languages. I think that the more we think about this, the stronger the articulation of Indigenous Knowledge will become.

I am half Cree and half Swedish—so I guess it is only natural for me to see similarities between Cree thinking, stories, and theory, and European ones. An example of an interesting overlap is between Cree storytelling and hermeneutics. Hans-Georg Gadamer speaks of how there are many possibilities of interpretation, depending on where one is situated. It is kind of like interpreting a sculpture in a gallery—depending on where you are standing, you will see different aspects. It is like that with stories—all of the old Cree storytelling masters understood that everyone would understand the stories slightly differently, depending on what the listener brought into the hearing of the story, each listener's "place of standing," the ground and experience that makes understanding possible.

itwêstamâkêwin 'translation'; literally, 'the process of speaking for someone else'. otitwêstamâkêw 'interpreter, translator'.

kiskinohtahikana 'signs'; literally, 'things that guide'.

nêhiyawâcimo-kiskisiwin 'Cree narrative memory'. I thought I would try to translate this, the title of one of my books.

môsihâcimowin 'feeling in the telling of a story' or 'narrative empathy'. The latter is a term I have coined in English during my teaching to get students to try to imagine being characters. I imagine that others have used this term—I think the idea behind it is very powerful.

ahkwêhtaw(astê)-nisitotamowin 'layering of interpretation' (the idea from hermeneutics).

kâ-âcimot 'narrator'; literally, 'one telling stories/news/âcimowina'.

kâ-âtayôhkêt 'narrator'; literally, 'one telling legends/sacred stories/âtayôhkêwina'.

itê ê-nisitohtamihk 'interpretative location'.

nisitohtamonâhk 'field of meaning'; literally, 'the land and territory of understanding'.

tawahikêyihtamowin 'theory'; literally, 'the process of creating space/room/paths with thinking'.

âniskwâcimowin 'intertextuality'.

ᐅᓂᐦᑳᐧ ᒋᒪᐃᐧᐤ

• • •

The idea of "text" is one of the key concepts in literary theory. I want
to open up the way we conceive of it. Instead of assuming a written
bias, I want to shift how we think about "text." A text is something
that stays the same over time; but of course our interpretation of that
text could shift. Perhaps one way to describe something that stays
the same over time (but does not imply "written culture") could
be tâpitawipayihcikan 'the thing that occurs in a similar fashion'.

DAY 84

BANNOCK

They may take our country, but they will not take our bannock! Oh, I guess they brought bannock, well, uhm…

The bannock forces have been awakened and angered. It is beyond description the grave error we have committed by not including a list about bannock before now. I hope that addressing the subject here will do a bit to correct our bad bannock karma.

Bannock is the mysterious force that binds all living things in the universe together. kayâs, a long time ago, there was an Old Cree Man, called Bannockin, who brought balance back to the previously unsettled bannock equilibrium, and whose actions ushered in a period of peace lasting until the great wars with the Blackfoot in the early 1800s.

Remember: never bring Wonder Bread to a pahkwêsi-*gun* fight. (*See* Day 65.)

pahkwêsikan 'bannock' (in some dialects, this also means 'bread'). My understanding of this stem is that pahkwêsikê is the verb that describes cutting pieces off (bread, bannock, etc.). Another stem is mâkonikê 'to knead bread'.

pîswêhkasikan 'bread' (in some dialects): pîswê- 'soft, fluffy'; -hkas- to bake; -ikê is the generic object—and so, together, this is 'to bake fluffy things' or 'fluffy-bake things'.

pimiy 'lard'. The Robin to the Batman of Bannock.

pahkwêsikanaskiy 'Scotland'. I am taking some dramatic liberties here, of course, but this is literally 'the land of bannock' (or scones, for that matter). I remember one time when I was eighteen, and someone said that bannock was from Scotland and was brought here in ships and kilts during the fur trade. I nearly decked him, saying that he was lying. I said, "The môniyâw took our land, do you want to take our bannock, too?" I settled down then, and eventually settled down to the tâpwêwin 'truth' that bannock does come from Scotland.

iyinito-pahkwêsikan 'baked bannock'; literally, 'the common, ordinary, or usual kind of bannock'. This term is used in order to distinguish between baked and fried bannock.

sâsâpiskisikê-pahkwêsikan 'fried bannock'. I remember back in the pre-disco days of the 1970s, nimosômipan John R. McLeod would make fried bannock sometimes for days at a time before big powwow hoka-fests in the Battlefords area. I remember the stacks of bannock getting higher and higher like a great wall of grease and hope. Then we would go to the powwow, and he would give it all away. I never really was much for powwow dancing myself, but those trips with my mosôm are some of the fondest memories that I have.

pahkwêsikanihkê 'to make bannock'; nihtâ-pahkwêsikanihkê- 'to make bannock well, to be known for baking good bannock'.

In the old days, this was a test to see whether a man would be a suitable husband.

pahkwêsikaniyiniwak 'the bannock people', the Crees.

opahkwêsikanimi- 'to have bannock'; kôpahkwêsikanimin cî? 'Got Bannock?'.

sômini-pahkwêsikan 'raisin bannock'.

wâkâsi-pahkwêsikan 'banana bannock'.

kôkôpahkisa-pahkwêsikan 'chocolate-chip bannock'.

pahkwêsikanis 'little piece of bannock'.

pahkwêsikan-wîhtikow a metaphorical way of saying 'someone who eats all of the bannock'.

êkwayâc kotawânâpiskohk ohci 'fresh out of the oven'.

kâya sâh-sêkisi, mow pahkwêsikan 'Don't fear, eat bannock'.

• • •

Back when I was at First Nations University, we had a weekly Cree conversational group that we wanted to jokingly call "Cree Toastmasters." But we got a nasty letter from Toastmasters International, or some such, telling us we couldn't use the name. So instead of "toastmasters," we settled on pahkwêsikan-okimâwak 'the bannock bosses'!

DAY 85

RUNNING

Today, I want to play and riff on the theme of running, as many Cree and Saulteaux were noted runners. I think of cistêmâwiyiniw (Tobacco Being) who lived in the Meadow Lake area. He would travel across rivers and tough terrain to deliver messages and news throughout the region. In a way, he, like other runners, could be thought of as an old kayâs ago newspaper.

pimipahtâ 'to run'; can also mean 'to run in an election': pim(i)- implies to 'move along, in a succession' or 'all actions in a succession'.

sôhkêpahtâ 'to run hard'.

nêstosipahtâ 'to run while tired; to tire oneself running'.

papâmipahtâ 'run around': papâmi- 'around'.

wâwâkikâtêpahtâ 'run bow-legged'.

napotokanêpahtâ 'run knock-kneed'.

sêsâwipahtâ 'to jog': sêsawî 'to exercise'.

wâsakâmêpahtâ 'to run around in a circle, run all the way around'.

nâspitâmo 'to run for cover'. This implies 'to flee for good, forever'.

kapâpahtâ 'to run to land, run out of the water': kapâ- denotes movement to shore. When I think of the stories of my late grandfather Gabriel Vandall, and his fight at Juno Beach during World War II, I think of how he and the other soldiers ran to shore—this verb would describe this well. I think that perhaps the battle of Juno Beach could be correctly described as kapâpahtâ-nôtinitowin 'the battle where people run to land from water'.

wayawîpahtâ 'to run outside'. Maybe there is a brushfire that gets out of control, and you have to yell to the dumb-ass who started it, "wayawîpahtâ boy! Put that fire out!"

natimipahtâ 'to run upriver'.

pitihkopahtâ 'run with a thudding noise'. The same stem is used for pitihko-sâkahikan 'Sounding Lake' and is also related to kâ-pitihkônâhk 'Thunderchild First Nation'.

kîwêpahtâ 'to run home'.

takopahtâ 'to arrive by running'.

sâkihipahtâ 'to run to love'.

DAY 86

POSTAGE

While compiling these lists of words, I found myself writing more and more kayâs-school letters, despite increasingly relying on e-mail and my iPhone. I think there is something about old-fashioned letters that we have lost, something that has to do with the time and care taken in writing them. You have to stop and think about what you are going to say, and, conversely, you sometimes need time to think about what your response to a letter will be. When we write letters, we also tend to keep them more than we do e-mails, which creates an archive of thoughts and experiences to be retrieved in the future. The following list brings together different words on this theme.

masinahikan asiwacikanis 'envelope'; literally, 'the writing thing that you put something inside' or 'letter-pocket'.

ayîsihcikan 'stamp'. In Anishinaabemowin: biijibiigan 'something like a letter you send'; gwaakizigaan 'something like a glue'.

pêtasinahikanis 'postcard'.

masinahikan-mistikowat 'mailbox'.

masinahikaniyiniw 'mailman'.

masinahikan-otâpânâsk 'mail truck'.

pêtasinahikê 'to send something by mail'.

pêtasinahikan 'something sent by mail'.

pêtasinahikêwikamik 'post office'.

kisî-itisahipayihtâkan 'express'; literally, 'the thing that is sent with great speed'.

tahkowatêw-masinahikan 'couriered letter'; literally, 'something that is carried on one's back', in reference to the courier.

DAY 87

GUNS

It is an old custom among the Crees to give away the guns of someone who has passed away. Often the guns were given to the deceased's old hunting buddies and those the person spent a great deal of time with in the bush. This practice exists to this day.

I thought it would be useful, because of the central role that guns have played in Cree life and culture, to spend some more time on terms relating to them. On Day 61, we looked at terms about hunting, which had some words about guns; this list continues where the other list left off, focussing particularly on guns.

pâskisikan 'gun'.

akocipâskisikanê 'put a gun on a gun rack': akoci- 'to hang', so literally, 'hanging a gun'.

akocipâskisikanâhtik 'gun rack': -âhtik 'something made of wood'.

kaskitêw 'gunpowder'; literally, 'black'.

nîmâskwân 'gun carried along with one'.

sîsîpokât 'gun hammer'; literally, 'duck leg'.

pâskisikanâhtik 'gun stock'.

pîhtâsowin 'the act of loading a gun'.

opâskisikani- 'have a gun'.

pâskis 'shoot [someone/game/bird, etc.] with a gun'.

pêyakwaskanôs 'single-barrelled gun'.

nîmipâskisikanê 'carry a gun on your person'.

macwêwês 'repeating gun, machine gun'; literally, 'the little sounder'. This is the diminutive of matwêwê- (VII) 'to detonate; sound heard in the distance'; and this term could also be rendered as matwêwê-pâskisikan. I remember my uncle, the late Burton Vandall, describing the Germans on Juno Beach as the "Shredders." Perhaps kîski-pâskisikan 'the cutting gun' could be used to describe this.

kotahâskwâs 'aim at [someone/game/bird, etc.]'.

DAY 88

INTERACTING WITH YOUR DOG

Dogs play a key role in Cree culture. At one time, before horses, dogs hauled our stuff, moved our tipis, carried our bannock, and licked our faces and made us feel better after a long day at the office battling our adversaries on the open plains.

There is a funny story I heard once. One time, a man was sitting in his sweat lodge, and he was praying. Going through various thanks-givings, the man opened his eyes after praying hard. ê-kî-tipiskâk ('it was dark'), aya ('but'), ê-kî-wâpi-wâstêk ('there was a white light'). "hâw, mosôm," itwêw ('"Hello, my mosôm," he said'). When he eventually opened the doors of the sweat lodge, his white dog came over and licked him in the face. wahwâ, atim! wahwâ!

Here are some words that would be helpful for interacting with your dog.

atim 'dog'.

atimonâhk 'dog park'; literally, 'the land or territory of dogs'.

nâcipahtâ 'fetch'; literally, 'get something by running'—good word!

api 'sit'.

mikisimo 'bark' (also miki).

oyôyo 'howl'. This can be used for wolves and coyotes, too, and maybe Crees outside of bingo with no sôniyâw.

atim-wâskahikan 'dog house'.

atim-oyâkan 'dog dish'.

atimotâpânêyâpiya 'dog harness'.

sakâpêkinikan 'dog leash'. The stem here is used for horses, but it would make sense if this were used for dogs, because dogs were important to Crees in the same way that horses were.

atimo-mîciwin 'dog food'.

kîkwây ôma? 'what is this?'.

tihtipî 'roll over'.

nayahcikêwatim 'pack dog'.

nakî 'stop' (a good word for dogs).

acimosis 'pup'.

nisihkâc pimohtê 'walk slowly'.

pasikô 'get up'.

kâwiya 'don't!' (I remember hearing my old relatives on Sandy Lake say this to me when I was a kid!).

ê-nêmot 'he growls'.

pâkâhtowân 'ball'; pâkâhcowânis 'little ball'.

pakitin 'let it go' (animate; for example, a ball); pakitina 'let it go' (inanimate; for example, a bone).

SWEETGRASS AS A YOUNG MAN (PART 2)

FROM *PLAINS CREE TEXTS*

Today, we revisit the *Plains Cree Texts* story of Sweetgrass that we first discussed on Day 45. Again, the narrator was kâ-kîsikâw-pîhtokêw ('Coming Day'). I find the vocabulary in these texts so interesting and so layered with both meaning and history. It is within these stories that we can retrieve a great deal of the classical vocabulary—vocabularly that I believe can enrich our view of the world today.

ihtasi- 'to be of such a number'. Here, it is referring to a war party.

mostohtê 'travel by foot'. It is interesting to note that Crees did not have an abundance of horses, and it was not uncommon for people to travel by foot—a key motivating factor for young men to try to "borrow" horses.

niyânanwâw ê-tipiskâyik 'when five nights had passed'. Note that the verb is in the present tense as is common in classical Cree narratives.

pâskisa 'shoot it (inanimate) with a gun'.

wiyanih 'skin and cut up an animal' (for example, a buffalo).

maskisin 'moccasin'.

mîsaha 'mend it' (for example, a moccasin).

ê-pîkopayiki 'they are worn, broken' (referring to the moccasins). The stem is pîkopayi-.

ê-ispatinâyik 'the land is hilly; it is hilly'. The verb is in the obviative form, implying that another third-person character in the story is also being referenced.

kisiwâk 'close; nearby'.

pitihkwê- 'to make a thudding sound'.

mostoswa mihcêt 'great heard of buffalo' (again with the buffalo marked as obviative).

ayâhciyiniwa mihcêt 'large band of Blackfoot' (obviative).

nawaswâta 'pursue something'.

DAY 90

COMPUTER
TERMINOLOGY

I think that it is important that the Cree language articulates contemporary experiences. We need to explore and document the realities that surround ourselves in the present, while drawing upon the words and imagery of our classical narratives and pakaski-nêhiyawêwin. We have examined some of the words below already, but I thought it would be good to bring all computer-related terms together under one concentrated heading.

I remember once I asked my uncle, the late Burton Vandall, about the word for computer. He told me that when he was working near La Ronge, Saskatchewan, the word they used was mamâhtâwi-âpacihcikan 'the tool that does amazing things'. The thing I take from this is that the organic development of the Cree language through time involves: first, organic creation of terms for contemporary things (such as this word for computer); and second, the attempt to coin words and see if these attempts at pushing old sonoric imagery make sense to speakers. In addition, we document (at least in a small way) the classical vocabulary.

mamâhtâwi-âpacihcikan 'computer'.

picikwâs-mamâhtâwi-âpacihcikan 'Apple computer'.

iyinito-mamâhtâwi-âpacihcikan 'PC'; literally, 'the regular or standard one'.

kiskisiwâhcikos 'memory stick'. My father used the stem -âhtik (or the diminutive -âhcikos) not just for wooden things but for anything bearing the morphology of a stick.

masinatahikan 'keyboard'; literally, 'the thing you type on'.

papaki-mamâhtâwi-âpacihcikanis 'iPad'; literally, 'the thin, little computer'.

âpakosîs 'mouse'.

naspitêyihtamowin 'digital'; literally, 'the thinking that is grounded in images and representations'.

masinahikêpicikan 'printer'; literally, 'the thing that "pulls" written words'.

kiskêyihtamowinâstan 'wireless'. I coined this as, literally, 'wind of knowledge', used to describe the way information moves through the air.

mamâhtâwi-âpacihcikanâspinêwin 'virus'; literally, 'a computer sickness'.

TRADITIONAL GAMES

Games and sports have always been very important ways of socializing. Below, we look at some traditional games as briefly described in David Mandelbaum's *The Plains Cree*. Some of these are still being played and others would certainly be worth reviving in modern competitions like the Inuit Games. Some of the spellings and even names are very tentative, so perhaps in the future someone might come forward with suggestions for improving the interpretations here.

Men's and Women's Games

ê-cikahkwêhk 'Stick-Dropping Game', although this term is also used for throwing darts.

ê-pâkâhtowêhk 'Playing with a Ball'. Mandelbaum described this as a game something like field hockey, but pâkâhtowêwin has also been used for lacrosse (Île-à-la-Crosse was so named because this game was played there), and today pâkâhtowêwin is commonly the word used to refer to soccer (that is, real football). I heard stories from R.J. Morin of how the Cree and Dene would have epic contests of this game at Île-à-la-Crosse. I hope that someday he puts together a book of these stories.

ê-kwâskwâskwênatowêhk 'Tossing the Ball'. kwâskwênatowê- is the word often used today to refer to playing football (that game the Saskatchewan Roughriders play).

tâpahwân 'Stringing the Bone Cups Game'—this is the Pin and Cup Game.

Men's Games

ê-pimotahkwâtahk 'Shooting Arrows'. It is interesting to note that many of the old Crees who were alive well into the twentieth century still preferred to hunt with bows and arrows. For instance, my friend John Quinney told me that his grandfather, Old Ben Quinney, used to hunt rabbits like this into the 1960s.

tihtipinatowân 'Rolling Game'—the hoop and pole (or dart) game.

ê-cihcipinacowêsihk 'Hoop Game'. Old-school neechie basketball. Well, maybe not quite.

micihcîhk 'Hand Game'. It is said that Crees and others who fled to the United States after the events of 1885 brought this game back to Canada when they felt it was safe to return. The game is still widely played in northern Alberta and northern Saskatchewan. Stakes can be high, and the spectators gallery can be full of sighs. Given the continued popularity of this game, it should not be surprising that neechies like to play poker today. There are many names for this traditional game and its various versions: kâ-nîswâskwahk 'Double Stick'; oskanihk 'Bone Game'; and misi-kâcikanak (this name for the Hand Game refers to the playing pieces that are hidden, often under the blanket, and moved around while songs are sung, to throw opponents off their game).

pakêsêwiyâkan 'Shaking Game'; but literally, the 'dice bowl': pakêsê- 'play dice'. I was thinking that maybe fuzzy dice could be called pakêsêhkâna 'fake dice'.

sôsimêwin 'Sliding Snow Darts'. sôsimân 'snow dart' is the common form of the dart used in this game, though Mandelbaum also gave the variant game and word sôskominân. The Haudenosaune have a similar game.

maskisinatowêwin 'The Moccasin Game'.

A Women's Game

ê-ohpwêpitisowayêhk 'The Testicle Game'. We'll just leave that to the imagination. Needless to say, it was a ball game. Sweet mother of Nanabush—not a game that some nâpêwak would enjoy watching.

WINTER SPORTS

For the 2010 Winter Olympic Games, APTN broadcast several sports with First Nations language commentary. Here is a sample of the terms they used, as developed at a vocabulary workshop facilitated by First Nations University and held in Prince Albert in 2009. Four Cree commentators from Saskatchewan participated: Barry Ahenakew, Abel Charles, Robert Merasty, and Harry Opikokew.

piponi-mêtawâniwan 'Winter Games'.

sôniskwâtahikêwin 'hockey'. I have always used the term 'skating' for 'hockey', so I am glad to learn this one. The derivation is a little uncertain, but I expect it has to do with 'ice' in some way.

sôniskwâtahikêwikamik 'hockey arena'.

sôniskwâtahikêwikamikohkânis 'table-top hockey'; literally 'a fake hockey arena'!

sôskwanâtahikêwin 'skating'.

sôskwanâtahikana 'skates'.

napakiwânis 'puck', clearly short for naPAKiwânis! Another word that has been used for puck is atihkwasiniy 'caribou stone'. Remember that môswasiniy 'moose stone' is a bullet (*see* Day 36).

pakamiskaw 'bodycheck him'. When compounding, the root pakam- implies a physical collision; rough contact. Consider pakamahw- 'to hit someone'.

ê-kînikwânipayihot 's/he does an axel jump'; literally, 's/he throws her/himself in a spiral'.

sôskwasinêwin 'curling'; literally, 'the sliding of stones'. My câpân used sôskwawêpinipicikê 'to hurl something by sliding'.

sôskwasiniy 'curling stone'.

sôskoyâpawiwin 'skiing'; literally, 'sliding while standing'.

kâ-ispâhkê-âpocikwânêcik 'freestyle aerials'; literally, 'those who do somersaults aloft'.

sôskwaciwêwin 'sledding'.

wîsko-sôskwaciwâkan 'bobsleigh'.

napakitâpânâsk 'toboggan': napaki- 'flat'; -tâpânâsk 'vehicle'.

wîhkwêtâpânâsk 'rounded toboggan': wîhkwê- and wîsko- 'rounded'; -tâpânâsk 'vehicle', referring to 'toboggan'.

DAY 93

SWEETGRASS AS A
YOUNG MAN (PART 3)

FROM *PLAINS CREE TEXTS*

With the following list, we continue to study the narration of kâ-kîsikâw-pîhtokêw ('Coming Day'), which we examined on Days 45 and 89. As noted previously, these stories were collected on the Sweetgrass Reserve (nakiwacîhk) in the 1920s and then published in 1934.

While some editing is necessary given today's orthography, what makes these narratives so important is that they were recorded with a great deal of accuracy and provide a window into the past in terms of how the nêhiyawak saw the world in the 1920s and the 1930s.

wâpamikoci ta-nipahikot 'if they saw him; they would kill him': wapam- 'see someone'; nipah- 'kill someone'. -ikot attached to both of these verbs indicates that the action is directed from one or more less topical participants ("they") toward the more topical third person in the story ("him"). In the first instance, the additional suffix -i (which changes the /t/ in -ikot to [c], that is, -ikoci) denotes a future conditional state of affairs, a possible happening.

apisîs ê-sakâsiyiki 'small clumps of trees'.

acosisa ê-tahkonahk 'he was carrying his arrows': acosisa 'arrows'; tahkona 'carry something'. In this instance, it seems that the word for 'arrow' is being treated as an inanimate noun, since the ending on the verb (-ahk) tells us that a third person is acting on an inanimate object. However, acosis 'arrow' is usually animate, so we might have expected the verb to be ê-tahkonât.

pimw- 'to shoot [someone]' (in this context, with an arrow).

otina 'to take [something]' (in this context, to take a gun). Many of you have heard a highly compressed form of this as na 'here, take it'.

mihcêt itê kâ-nipahâyit mostoswa 'where they killed many buffalo'. The text does not articulate the manner in which the buffalo were killed.

âta wiya wî-maskamêw 'he wanted to rob them': maskam- 'to rob, to take [something animate]'; âta wiya 'though, although, nonetheless, anyway'. Note: here, the wî- denotes a desire or wish (whereas today this often denotes a future action in general). I have noted that the Anishinaabe here use wî- in a similar fashion; almost like how contemporary Plains Cree uses nôhtê-.

ê-kostahk ta-nisitawêyimikot ê-nêhiyâwit 'he was afraid to be recognized as a Cree'. Note: Cree ta- *plus* a verb functions in an analogous fashion to the English infinitive 'to'.

piyisk miyâskawêw 'finally, he passed them': piyisk 'finally'; miyâskaw- (VTA) 'to pass someone'. I have heard this used in the context of vehicle travel. Note: a related word, miyâskam, means 'past or after' in relation to time. For example, nîsitanaw cipahikanisa miyâskam nîso tipahikan means 'twenty minutes past two o'clock'.

namôya kiskêyihtam kwayask an interesting way to say 'unknowingly' or 'unwittingly'; literally, 'he didn't know for sure'. It's not that the Cree verb functions as an adverb. This verbal construction in Cree simply requires an adverb when translated into English.

wiyanih- 'to prepare; to skin and cut up' (in this context, buffalo). Here I assume that it means 'to butcher'. Could a contemporary butcher be called wiyanihikês (or perhaps wiyanihcâkês)?

sakâpêkin- 'to lead someone by the reins'. mistahi-maskwa famously used this verb to metaphorically describe how he didn't want to be led along like a horse by the newcomers, namôya ê-wî-sakâpêkinikawiyân, using old Cree images to describe colonialism. (*See* Day 38.)

apisîs ohpimê 'off to the side'.

pimohtê although used today for 'to walk', it was often used in *Plains Cree Texts* for 'riding a horse'; could it be inferred that the walking is that of a horse?

SWEETGRASS AS A YOUNG MAN (PART 4)

FROM *PLAINS CREE TEXTS*

Today's list completes the exploration of the narrative that we have studied on Days 45, 89, and 93.

têpwê 'to let out a whoop'; 'yell'.

pê-sipwêpayi 'to start off in the direction of the speaker': pê- generally indicates motion toward the speaker, while sipwê- means 'leave, set off'. These might appear contradictory when used together, but the actor must have set off (from his/her current location) in the direction of the speaker.

nawaswât- 'to pursue someone'. The stem form here is never used as a word by itself. As a command, the form would be nawaswâs! 'pursue him/her!'.

ayahciyiniw nawaswâtêw ôhi nêhiyawa, ê-wî-kakwê-nipahât 'the Blackfoot pursues the Cree to try to kill him'. The conjunct mode here has been translated as an infinitive according to English dictates, but it might be closer to something like 'as he was going to try to kill him'. There are two layers of future conditionality in this sentence: wî- is a future tense marker—in classical Cree, it seems to denote a desire (as in Anishinaabemowin); kakwê- 'attempt' indicates a possible state of affairs.

mahti kisiwâk kit-âyât 'I will let him get closer'.

ê-askôkot 'he was pursuing him'. The main character of the story is being pursued by someone else.

wâyinîpit- 'to turn back a horse' (that is, pull him back around). Again, this is a stem form that is never actually used as a word itself. The command form would be wâyinîpis! 'pull him back around!'. The stem wâyinî- has many variant pronunciations across dialects, so it may also sound like wâwonî- or wâyinô-.

môskîstaw- 'to attack someone', 'charge at someone'.

patahw- 'to miss someone with a shot'. Note the /w/ in this VTA stem will drop at the end of a word, as when the verb is used as a command: êkâwiya patah! 'Don't miss him!'. But it shows up in other forms, such as kî-patahwêw 'he missed him'.

nîhciwêpahw- 'to knock someone off' (in this context to knock someone off a horse). This is another of those VTA stems with the disappearing /w/.

otihta 'reach a specific point'.

pôyo 'stop'.

asawâpi 'scout, look out'. I remember Wes Fineday once used this metaphor to discuss artists. When he said this, the image left a great impression on me, and I think of it to this day. It can also mean 'to watch', as in being a lookout for approaching people, visitors, enemies, or even game.

DAY 95

HALLOWE'EN

I remember one time a Cree kid came to the door on Hallowe'en. ê-matwêhikêt ('He knocked on the door'). nôhtâwiy ê-kî-yôhtênahk iskwâhtêm ('My late dad opened the door'). The neechîsis ('the little neechie') in his Hallowe'en regalia said the magic words: "Trick or Treat." nôhtâwîpan ê-kî-miyât pakâna ('Dad gave the little neechîsis peanuts'). In a voice laden with disgust and disappointment, the nâpêsis said, "Ever cheap," and abruptly turned and closed up the open space of his pillowcase. "wahwâ," nôhtâwîpan itwêw ('"Holy smokes!" my late father said'.)

I hear that that little neechie went on to become a bingo caller in northern Ontario. Life is a strange circle indeed.

cîpay-kîsikâw 'Hallowe'en'; literally, 'ghost day'.

môhcowi-kîsikâw 'Hallowe'en'; literally, 'the day of fooling around'.

ka-wayêsihitin êkâ cî ka-miyin sîwihcikanis 'trick or treat'; literally, 'I'll trick/deceive you, or you'll give me some candy';

ka-nanâtohkohitin êka cî ka-miyin maskihkîs 'I'll joke or tease you, or you'll give me candy (literally, 'the little medicine')'.

sîwihcikanisiwat 'pillowcase [to hold candy]'; literally, 'candy bag'.

misi-mînis 'pumpkin'; literally, 'big berry'. But another word that is used is osâwipak; literally, 'orange/yellow plant'. The plural is osâwipakwak.

kaskitê-minôs 'black cat'.

kostâcisîhowin 'Halloween costume'; literally, 'dressing scarily'. Also, môhcohkân-ayiwinisa, literally, 'the fooling clothes' or 'clown clothes'.

sôkâw-kîskwêpayiwin 'sugar rush'.

osâwipak kâ-masinihkotiht 'Jack O'Lantern'; literally, 'pumpkin carved with designs'.

maskihkîs 'candy'; literally, 'little medicine' (this has also been used specifically for chocolate). Also, sîwihcikanisa, literally, 'small sweetened things'; and sîwanosa or sîwâsa, literally, 'small sweet things'.

cîpay oskana 'skeleton'; literally, 'ghost's bones'. Also, miyawikana, literally 'body bones'.

DAY 96

INTERACTING WITH OUR CHILDREN (PART 4): BEDTIME

Children are the future of the language, are our living past, and their bodies and souls are the vessels of our culture. It is important that we talk Cree to them in every way we know.

I think it makes a big difference if we put our children to bed in a gentle way—so they can end the day in a positive manner. The use of Cree terminology can definitely help that process.

taswêkastâ 'spread it' (in this context, a blanket).

pakâsimo 'take a bath'. Be careful not to confuse this word with pakâso 'to boil'. I once heard a story of a Cree woman who, while talking on the phone to an older relative, wanted to tell her relative that the children were having a bath. ayâyk (as my late dad would say), the relative then accidently said pakâso in the place of pakâ-simo! I imagine that Old Woman said, "wahwâ!"

ayamihtamawin 'read it to me'.

ayamihtamaw 'read it to him or her'.

ayamihcikêstamaw awâsis 'read to the child'.

tipiskâw-wâstênikan 'night light'.

nipêwayâna 'pyjamas'; literally, 'sleep clothes'.

akohp 'blanket'.

kakêkina masinahikan 'choose a book'.

kâsîhkwê 'wash your face'.

kisîpêkâpitêhon, kisîpêkinâpitêwâkan 'toothbrush'.

kisîpêkâpitêho 'brush one's teeth'.

tipiskâw 'it is dark; it is night'.

kâya mêtawê wayawîtamihk 'don't play outside' (when it is dark).

aspiskwêsimon 'pillow'.

mîciwinis 'snack'.

DAY 97

BEDTIME FOR THE BINGO CALLER

After a long night (kinwês 'a long time') of bingo calling, any bingo caller needs to be able to kick back, relax, and have a good sleep. Here are some more words, building on the last day's list, for nighttime—sleeping—and relaxing before bed.

nêsto-têpwê 'be tired from calling [bingo]'.

aywêpisi 'rest; take a little break'.

pawâta 'dream; dream about something'.

paskina 'fold [a blanket] open or over'.

wêwêkisini 'lay curled up wrapped in your blanket'.

awasitê itisini 'push over; lay further away'.

-hkwâmi 'sleeping'. This stem must be compounded with a stem in front to describe the manner of sleep (as seen in the next four words).

sâsâkisitêhkwâmi 'sleep with your feet sticking out'.

kitowêhkwâmiw 's/he sleeps loudly' (that is, snoring).

nâspitihkwâmiw 's/he sleeps for a long period of time'. This can also be used for being in a coma, or for a neechie Sleeping Beauty.

osâmihkwâmi 'to oversleep'.

DAY 98

GIVING STRENGTH

Today I would like to take an in-depth look at the root maskaw-, the use of which implies that something has an element of strength.

I remember that my late father, Jermiah McLeod, remarked that this was a key way to think about the philosophy of Cree—and the meaning of Cree words. The meanings of the roots and stems, and also the way in which we combine these elements, is at the heart of the Cree language.

maskawistikwânê 'to be stubborn'; literally, 'to have a hard or strong head'. I remember my father taught me this word about twenty years ago.

maskawisî 'to be strong'. I remember in the classical Cree story of pîkahin okosisa, this term was used by the late Bill Stonestand in his telling of the story. He said that pîkahin okosisa was sent to show that the môniyâwak 'newcomers' were not more maskawisîwak than the Creator. It is through this little part of the story that I remember this word.

ê-maskawâkonakâk 'hard snow; packed snow'.

maskawâpisk 'strong metal'.

maskawastâ 'place something strongly, firmly'.

maskawâw 'it is hard'.

maskawêkin 'a strong or durable fabric or cloth'. This word could be used for the heavy canvas for a painting.

maskawêyiht- 'to think strongly; to be firm; to have clear ideas'. This is one of the greatest things my late father taught me.

maskawihkomân 'strong or hard knife'.

maskawisîhcikê 'to make things strong, to strengthen things'.

maskawisîhtâ 'make something strong, to strengthen something'; this could apply to a military or tactical position.

maskawisîwin 'strength'. I remember hearing people use this word in prayers: mahti miyin maskawisîwin.

CONTEMPORARY WARFARE

I have always been interested in Cree and Cree-Métis narratives of warfare because so many of my relatives were soldiers, including Gabriel Vandall. I wrote a book of poems about him, and the stories about him. Below, I have gathered some words about warfare, and I hope you will find these interesting. I find the relationships between these more contemporary narratives of warfare and those found in *Plains Cree Texts* very interesting.

misti-pâskisikan 'tank'; also nôtinikêwin-tâpânâsk, literally 'war truck', and simâkanisihkân-otâpânâsk, literally 'soldier vehicle'.

mônahikana 'trenches'. sôniyâw-mônahikê means 'to mine for minerals', but the stem here does not specifically involve minerals. There was a great Cree leader by the name of kâ-mônahikos—and through his story the town of Medicine Hat got its name. In the story kâ-mônahikos digs into the ground and moves through the earth to escape the Blackfoot.

pahkisikan-âpacihcikan 'artillery'; literally, 'the exploding tool'.

macwêwê-pâskisikan 'machine gun'; also kâ-sôhkêkotêk pâskisikan, literally 'the gun that goes fast'.

simâkanisihkân 'soldier'; literally, an 'imitation soldier', apparently marking a semantic shift with the -hkân ending to denote new ways of doing things. simâkanisihkân-askiy refers to the Treaty land in Sutherland in Saskatoon held by Muskeg Lake.

nôtinikê-âpacihcikana 'war tools'. This word encompasses all the machines that are used in war.

simâkanisihkânisîhowin 'uniform'; literally, 'soldier uniform'.

tâwahw- 'to pierce someone with a shot' (VTA).

simâkanisikimâw 'commanding officer'.

kipahwâkan 'prisoner'.

DAY 100

UNTIL NEXT TIME

Putting together the lists of terms for this book has been an interesting journey. mitoni ê-miyo-papâmipiciyahk ôta nêhiyawêskanâhk ('It has been a good journey, on this Cree road'). mistahi kî-ispayin ('Much has happened'). mihcêtiwak kiwâhkômâkaninawak ê-kî-kîwêcik, tâpiskôc Freda Ahenakewipan êkwa mîna nôhtawîpan ('Many of our relatives have gone home, such as the late Freda Ahenakew and my late father'). ispîhk ê-kakwê-kânawêyihtamahk kipîkiskwêwininaw, kikistêyimânawak ('When we work to hold onto our language, we honour them').

This is the last entry of this cycle. Again, it has been a good journey, and I hope that the efforts have inspired you, even in a small way, to learn more of the Cree language.

It is not inevitable that Indigenous languages pass away like a dying fire—we can keep them alive if we use them every day, to the best of our ability. And we have to help each other learn them, and support each other in doing so.

nêhiyawêtân 'let's speak Cree'.

ê-nêhiyawêmototâtoyahk 'we speak Cree to each other'.

sêsâwîtân 'let's practice'; literally, 'let's exercise'.

mahti nêhiyawêmototawin 'please speak Cree to me'.

kiyokêwin 'visiting': the backbone of Cree culture and language.

kâya pakicî 'don't give up'; also âhkamêyimo 'continue on'.

kiskinwahamâkosi mitâtaht itwêwina tahto kîsikâw 'learn ten words a day'.

iskwayikohk iyiniwak ê-nêhiyawêcik, nêhiyawêwin ka-sôhkêpayin 'As long as there are people who speak Cree, the language will be strong'.

mahti wîcihitotân ka-nêhiyawêyahk 'Let's help each other speak Cree'.

iskwayikohk pitamâ 'until next time'.

GUIDE TO CREE PRONUNCIATION

AROK WOLVENGREY

nêhiyawêwin (Cree) is written in this book following the Standard Roman Orthography (SRO). It is "roman" in the sense that the symbols used are those of the Latin or Roman alphabet, but not necessarily applied in the same way that most readers will be used to from English. This is because the system behind this "orthography" is the sound system of the Cree language, for which it was expressly devised. Finally, it is "standard" in the sense that it captures not just the sounds (phones) of Cree, which can be quite variable across dialects, but also features of the structure of the language in order to provide a writing system that can be of use across all the variable dialects of Cree as spoken from Alberta through Ontario and beyond. Nevertheless, some modifications do occur within this standard to more closely represent specific dialects, and readers from different dialect areas will undoubtedly have variable pronunciations for many of the words in this book. The standard spelling unites and presents a key to the underlying meaning of these words.

The dialect most commonly represented in this book is southern Plains Cree, as spoken in south and central Saskatchewan and central Alberta. In this dialect, there are 17 distinct sounds, represented by 17 distinct symbols, alphabetized as follows:

a â c ê h i î k m n o ô p s t w y

There are 10 consonants and 7 vowels, with the vowels divided by the important feature of vowel length such that long vowels are marked by a circumflex (e.g., â, ê, î, ô) while short vowels are unmarked (e.g., a, i, o). Other symbols familiar to you from English simply do not and should not occur in Cree spelling. In fact, though there are some similarities to English sounds, it is important to note that even the 17 symbols in use do not always match their English equivalents and one must read Cree based on the rules of the Cree sound system. In other words, it is best to forget what you know about English. *nêhiyawêwin ôma* ('This is Cree'). Still, in the following pronunciation guide, examples will be given in square brackets [] to suggest a more English-based pronunciation to help you begin to learn Cree spelling and pronunciation. As always, however, it is best to learn your pronunciation from fluent speakers.

VOWELS

The vowel symbols used to represent Cree tend to provide English readers with the most surprises, since the vowels follow their more common assignments in the majority of languages of the world— in contrast to English. As already mentioned, and unlike English, vowel length is important for Cree, with long vowels marked by a circumflex (e.g., â). The seven vowels of Cree are as follows:

Short Vowels

a   - sounds like English "a" in "<u>a</u>bout" and "u" in "<u>u</u>p" (but certainly not the "u" of such words as "unique" or "put"; the English "u" symbol is never used for writing Cree). Examples include <u>a</u>w<u>a</u>s [uh WUS] 'go away' and <u>a</u>y<u>a</u>piy<u>a</u>k [uh YUP pee yuk] 'nets'.

i   - sounds like English "i" in "<u>i</u>n" or "f<u>i</u>t," never as in English "fine" or "fight." Examples include <u>nisit</u> [nis SIT] 'my foot' and <u>micimin</u> [MITS tsim min] 'hold him/her'.

o   - sounds like the English "o" in "<u>o</u>ccasion" or the "oo" of "b<u>oo</u>k", or the "u" of "p<u>u</u>t." Note the many different ways that this sound is spelled in English. In Cree, this sound is *o*, and only *o*. Examples include <u>o</u>k<u>o</u>t [oo KOOT] 'his/her nose' and <u>o</u>spit<u>o</u>n [OOS pit toon] 'his/her arm' (remembering to pronounce the "oo" like in "book," not as in "boot").

Long Vowels

â   - sounds something like the "a" in "f<u>a</u>" (as when singing "do, re, me, **fa**, so, la, ti, do"). As the long counterpart to short *a*, it is actually not a sound commonly found in most dialects of English. If, however, you were to pronounce "father" with an Irish accent, this would be much closer to the Cree sound than most English pronunciations of "father." Examples include *âhâsiw* [AA haa sew] 'crow' and *mâmaskâc* [MAA muss kaats] 'amazing; surprising'.

î   - sounds like the English "i" in "mach<u>i</u>ne," never as in "sh<u>i</u>ne." This so-called "e" sound has so many different spellings in

English (for example: e, ee, ea, ei, eo, ie, i, y, etc.), but one and only one in Cree: *î*. It is the long counterpart to short *i*. Examples include *sîsîp* [see SEEP] 'duck' and *nîkânîw* [NEE gaa nee-oo] 's/he leads, s/he is in front'.

ô — usually sounds like the English "o" in "s<u>o</u>" or "oa" in "b<u>oa</u>t" (or better yet, "oo" in German *Boot* 'boat'). It can, however, vary in pronunciation, so that some speakers may use a sound closer to English "oo" in "m<u>oo</u>se." Regardless, these two variant sounds do not represent an important, meaning-altering difference in Cree, and a single symbol is all that is needed. Long *ô* is the counterpart of short *o*. Examples include *môswa* [moh SWUH] 'moose' and *tôtamôh* [TOH tum moh] 'make him/her do it!'.

ê — sounds like the English "ay" in "h<u>ay</u>" or "ai" in "m<u>ai</u>n." This sound has no short counterpart. It must not be confused with the English "ee" sound or the Cree *î* sound. Examples include Swampy Cree *êhê* [AY HAY] 'yes' and *ê-sêwêyêk* [ay SAY way yayk] '(as) you (all) ring (as when wearing bells)'.

The vowel *ê* has been variably written with (ê) or without (e) the circumflex. As it is a long vowel, use of the circumflex here is consistent with the other long vowels. Even more importantly, the circumflex on *ê* is a way to indicate that this is the Cree vowel *ê*, not the English "e" which is so easily confused with the Cree *î* sound. This is particularly important across Cree dialects, since not all dialects use the *ê* sound. In Woods Cree and northern Plains Cree, all *ê* sounds have shifted to collapse with and be pronounced the same as *î*. Thus, where southern Plains and Swampy Cree speakers will say (and write) *kîwê* [kee WAY] 'go home', northern Plains and Woods Cree speakers will say *kîwî* [kee WEE]. It is perfectly acceptable to write this as *kîwê* or, for northern Plains and Woods Cree writers, *kîwî*—but "kêwê" (or "kewe") is simply incorrect, as no dialect pronounces this word like [kay WAY].

Stress

Throughout this guide so far, you will note that two-syllable words (e.g., *nisit* [nis SIT], *kîwê* [kee WAY]) have a main stress on the last syllable (shown by the use of capital letters in the pronunciation guide), while words of three or more syllables (e.g., *âhâsiw* [AA haa sew], *ayapiyak* [uh YUP pee yuk]) tend to have a main stress on the third last syllable. This is a fairly regular rule of Plains Cree, though exceptions may be encountered. It is also important to note that vowel length does not vary based on the stress pattern of Cree. A long vowel must stay long and a short vowel cannot be lengthened regardless of the presence or absence of stress. It is not uncommon, however, for short vowels (especially *i*) to be dropped altogether when in an unstressed position. This is the reason why *tânisi* [TAAN sih] 'how; hello' is written as if it were commonly pronounced with three syllables rather than two. The stress pattern clearly shows that this is a three-syllable word (constructed by combining the question element *tân-* with *isi* 'manner, way'), but it usually loses the middle syllable because of the deletion of the unstressed *i* (i.e., /TAA nis sih/ > [TAAN sih]).

CONSONANTS

There are ten consonants in most western dialects of Cree. Some are quite similar to English pronunciation, while others require more practice. The consonants are listed here in their alphabetical order, though certain sounds pattern more like one another (for instance, you will see that the explanations of *k*, *p*, *t* [and *c*] are all quite similar and require particular attention).

c — varies in pronunciation. In many areas of Plains Cree, it is pronounced like the "ts" in the English word "ca<u>ts</u>." In other dialects, it may be closer to the English "ch" or "tch" sound in "<u>ch</u>at" or "ca<u>tch</u>." This is a fact about each dialect, but the variation is not an issue for the Cree language as a whole. No meaning difference depends on the variation of "ts" and "ch" in Cree, which is to say that no pairs of Cree words will differ solely by an alternation of "ts" and "ch" sounds. Thus, only one symbol is needed and the digraph "ch" is never used. Furthermore, "c" is never used to represent a "k" sound, like it does in "<u>c</u>ook," or an "s" sound, as in "<u>c</u>ent," or both of these sounds in words like "<u>c</u>ir<u>c</u>us" or "<u>c</u>ir<u>c</u>le." One symbol for the one important sound. Like the consonants *k*, *p*, and *t* described below, *c* is not followed by a puff of air (or "aspiration"). Examples include *nîso<u>c</u>ih<u>c</u>* [NEE soo tseehts] or [NEE soo cheehch] "two fingers; two inches' and *<u>c</u>êh<u>c</u>apiwinis* [tsayh tsup POO win nis] or [chayh chup POO win nis] 'little chair'.

h — is similar to English "h" in sound, but it patterns quite differently. In English, "h" tends to start words or occur as a puff of air (aspiration) after consonants like "k," "p," or "t." In Cree, *h* very rarely begins words (with the exception of interjections like *hay hay* ["high high"] 'thanks' or *hâw* [how] 'all right') and never occurs as aspiration, but instead tends to occur only between vowels (e.g., *âhâsiw* [AA haa sew] 'crow') or at the end of syllables before consonants (as "pre-aspiration"; e.g., *aski<u>h</u>k* [us KEEHK] 'kettle, pail', *pêhtam* [payh TUM] 's/he hears it') or at the end of words (e.g., *wîcih* [wee TSIH] 'help him/her!'). When it occurs before consonants, *h* also tends to have a range of effects on the preceding vowel (see below). These features are very different from how "h" is used in English and is difficult for English speakers to adapt to. *h* is also quite variable within Cree dialects, ranging from a strongly articulated, almost rasping, puff of air in some dialect areas to completely silent in other dialects. For dialects where the sound is silent, the spelling is equivalent to the silent "gh" in English, but nevertheless useful in distinguishing the meaning of words.

k   - is pronounced like the sound in English "s**k**ill." Its sound is somewhere between the "k" in "**k**ill" and the "g" in "**g**ill," but is unlike English "k" in that it is never followed by a puff of air (or "aspiration"). The exact quality may vary between what sounds like English "k" and "g" sounds, with a more "g"-like sound most frequent between vowels. However, this is not an important difference in Cree: no pair of words will ever differ in Cree by interchanging these sounds. Thus, only one of the symbols is necessary. If in doubt, use *k*. "g" is never used. Examples include *kâkwa* [kaa KWUH] and *kîkinâhk* [KEE kin naahk] 'at our home'.

m   - is pronounced like the "m" in English "**m**umps." Examples include *mînom* [mee NOOM] 'correct him/her verbally' and *mamihcimo* [mum MEEH tsim moo] 'brag'.

n   - is pronounced like the "n" in English "**n**one." Examples include *nîpin* [nee PIN] 'summer' and *ninîkânînân* [nin nee GAA nee naan] 'we are in the lead'.

p - is pronounced like the sound in English "spill." Its sound is somewhere between the "p" in "pill" and the "b" in "bill," but is unlike English "p" in that it is never followed by a puff of air (or "aspiration"). As with *k*, the Cree *p* sound may vary between the two English sounds, but the difference is not important for Cree. It is an English artifact and not one that we need to pay attention to. If in doubt, use *p*. "b" is never used. Examples include *pîsim* [pee SIM] 'sun' and *asapâp* [US sup paap] 'thread'.

s - is generally pronounced like the "s" in English "suits." However, since there is no distinction in western Cree dialects between the "s" and "sh" sounds, some speakers might use a pronunciation somewhat closer to the English "sh" sound, especially in particular words (e.g., *nimosôm* [NIM moo sohm] or [NIM moo shohm] 'my grandfather'). Examples include *sîpîsis* [SEE pee sis] 'creek, stream' and *sasâkisîs* [sus SAAK cease] or [sus SAA kiss cease] 'stingy, stingy person'.

t - is pronounced like the sound in English "still." Its sound is somewhere between the "t" in "till" and the "d" in "dill," but is unlike English "t" in that it is never followed by a puff of air (or "aspiration"). Again, the Cree *t* sound may vary between the two English sounds, but the difference is not important for Cree. If in doubt, use *t*. "d" is never used. Examples include *tânitê* [TAAN tay] 'where' and *itôtamâtok* [(it) toh TUM maa took] 'do it for one another!'.

w - is pronounced like the "w" in English "way" and "wow." *w* also tends to have a range of effects on preceding vowels (see below). Examples include *wahwâ* [wuh WAA] 'Oh my!'

and _wâsêyâwiskwêw_ [waa say YOW wis kwayoo] 'Shining Woman'.

y   - is pronounced like the "y" in English "<u>y</u>es" and "<u>yay</u>." _y_ also tends to have a range of effects on preceding vowels (see below). Examples include _yôtin_ [yoh TIN] 'it is windy' and _yêhyêw_ [yayh YAY-OO] or [yay YAY-OO] 's/he breathes'. Note, however, that many instances of _y_ in Plains Cree change across the dialects. For instance, the examples just given would change the _y_ to _n_ in Swampy Cree (e.g., _nôtin_, _nênêw_) and to _th_ [ð] in Woods Cree (e.g., _thôtin_, _thîthîw_). For this reason, Plains Cree is sometimes called the Y-dialect, Swampy Cree is the N-dialect, and Woods Cree is the TH-dialect (with a "th" sound like in English "<u>th</u>is" or "<u>th</u>at," not like in "<u>th</u>in" or "wi<u>th</u>"). In fact, the reverse is more accurate since the name "Plains Cree" is used to indicate all dialects that use the _y_ in words like _yôtin_ regardless of whether they are spoken on the plains or prairie, or in the woodland, boreal forest, etc. One word of caution, though: not all _y_ sounds change across the dialects, so it can be difficult to know which Plains Cree _y_ sounds or Swampy Cree _n_ sounds will change. If you hear a Woods Cree word with a _th_ sound, though, you can be sure it will be _y_ in Plains and _n_ in Swampy (assuming the same word is used).

VOWELS AND CONSONANTS COMBINED

Finally, it is important to note that some consonants affect the way that some vowels are pronounced. Most importantly, when the vowels occur next to one of the three consonants known as "glides" or "semi-vowels" (**h**, **w**, **y**), various modifications can occur in the pronunciation of the basic vowel sounds.

h   - the effect of an "h-consonant" cluster (hC or "pre-aspirated" consonants, where "C" stands for any consonant, e.g., **hp**, **ht**, **hc**, **hk**; see below) on the preceding vowel can vary across dialects. In some areas, the distinction between long and short vowels is neutralized. In other words, it is usually very difficult, if not impossible, to tell the difference between long and short vowels before a combination of **h** and another consonant. Before hC, long and short vowels seem to merge into a single vowel which is short in duration, but closer to the quality of the long vowel. Hence:

- **ahC** and **âhC** both sound as in English "f<u>a</u>" (like **â**), but shorter in duration (like **a**).
- **ihC** and **îhC** both sound as in English "b<u>ea</u>t" (like **î**), but shorter in duration (like **i**).
- **ohC** and **ôhC** both sound as in English "b<u>oa</u>t" (like **ô**), but shorter in duration (like **o**).

In other dialects, the **h** is disappearing completely before consonants, in which case the preceding vowel tends to be lengthened. Hence:

- **ahC** and **âhC** both sound like **âC**.
- **ihC** and **îhC** both sound like **îC**.
- **ohC** and **ôhC** both sound like **ôC**.

Furthermore, in some dialects the **hk** cluster in particular is being lost at the end of words. Thus, words like *sâka-hikanihk* 'at the lake', which ends in the locative *-ihk* suffix may be pronounced as [saa guh HIG gun neehk], [saa guh HIG gun neek], or [saa guh HIG gun nih] depending on region. The *-hk* spelling at the end of such a word may then be completely silent for some speakers, but its presence in spelling is an important indicator of the locative meaning of the word.

w   - when following a vowel, **w** often sounds something like the short **o** or long **ô** vowels. It is very similar to these vowels for they are all similar in the place and manner in which they are produced in the mouth, including "rounding" of the lips. **w** has the following effects:

- **aw** is pronounced as in Canadian English "ab<u>out</u>."
- **âw** is pronounced as in English "w<u>ow</u>." But please note, it is never spelled "ow" in Cree. Cree **ow** will sound like a long **ô** (see below).
- **êw** is pronounced like a combination of English "ay-oo," and hence the common attempt to spell Cree words like *nâpêw* 'man' as "Napayo" in English.
- **iw** varies in pronunciation across dialects, from a sound similar to that in English "<u>new</u>" to the sounds of Cree short **o**, or long **ô**. The **w** effectively "rounds" the vowel, making it sound more like the round vowels (**o** and **ô**).
- **îw** is pronounced like a combination of English "ee-oo."
- **ow** is pronounced very much as in English "kn<u>ow</u>," and it is difficult to tell the difference between short **o**

and long *ô*. Before *w*, both vowels sound long. By spelling convention, when no dialect-internal means are available for determining the length of the vowel before *w*, the vowel is spelled as short *o* (e.g., *manitow* 'spirit', *ôhow* 'owl'). Such examples are found mostly in nouns.

- *ôw* is pronounced very much as in English "kn<u>ow</u>," and it is difficult to tell the difference between short *o* and long *ô*. Before *w*, both vowels sound long.

y

- when following a vowel, *y* often has a quality much like the short *i* or long *î* vowels, since these vowels and *y* are very similar in the place and manner in which they are produced in the mouth. In nouns and names, *y* usually only follows short vowels, and it has the following effects:

- *ay* is pronounced as in Canadian English "b<u>i</u>te." This spelling tends to be one of the most difficult for English speakers to adjust to. It is not the English "ay" in "d<u>ay</u>," but is instead closer to the sound in "<u>I</u>" or "<u>eye</u>."

- *iy* sounds very much like the long *î*, and it is not possible to tell the difference between short *i* and long *î* before *y*. Before *y*, both vowels sound long. By spelling convention, where no dialect-internal means are available for determining the length of the vowel before *y*, the vowel will always be spelled as a short *i* (e.g., *asiniy* 'stone'; *niya* 'I, me' [cf. Woods Cree *nîtha*]). Such examples are mostly found in nouns (and, as a side effect, the "iy" spelling at the end of words can be used to signal the occurrence of a noun in opposition to any other part of speech.

- *oy* is pronounced very much like the sound in English "b<u>oy</u>" or "b<u>uoy</u>."

In general, because the "semi-vowels" are so close to vowel sounds themselves, they are often involved in contractions. For example, a sequence like /ihi/ in *kisâkihitin* 'I love you' can be pronounced quite carefully (e.g., [kiss saa KIH hit tin]) or contracted (e.g., [kiss saa KEEH tin]). Such contractions are fairly predictable, but vary considerably in the speech of a single speaker or speakers in the same community, let alone across dialects. The Standard Roman Orthography therefore does not typically take into account contractions in rapid speech no matter how common they might be. Again, the best resource for learning proper pronunciation in any given area is to listen to the language as it is actually spoken.

ABOUT THE AUTHOR

Of Cree and Swedish ancestry, Neal
McLeod grew up on the James Smith
Cree Nation in Saskatchewan. He is
an associate professor of Indigenous
Studies at Trent University, a poet, a
painter, and the editor of *Indigenous
Poetics in Canada*.